Beowulf and the Appositive Style

Beowulf
and the
Appositive Style

BY FRED C. ROBINSON

THE UNIVERSITY OF TENNESSEE PRESS
KNOXVILLE

Publication of this book has been aided by a grant from The Better English Fund, established by John C. Hodges at The University of Tennessee, Knoxville.

Cloth: first printing, 1985; second printing, 1987.
Paper: first printing, 1987; second printing, 2015.

Frontispiece: From the Legendary of Cîteaux; Dijon, Bibliothèque Municipale. Tome IV, MS. 641, f. 7v; 12th century.

Library of Congress Cataloging in Publication Data

Robinson, Fred C.
    Beowulf and the appositive style.

    (The Hodges lectures)
    Includes index.
    1. Beowulf.   2. Anglo-Saxon language—Apposition.
3. Anglo-Saxon language—Style.   4. Christianity in
literature.   5. Paganism in literature.   I. Title.
II. Series.
PR1588.R6   1985   829.3   84-11889
ISBN 0-87049-444-9 (alk. paper)
ISBN 0-87049-531-3 (pbk.: alk. paper)

CONTENTS

PREFACE TO THE 2015 EDITION

Since the publication of *Appositive Style* studies of the style and theme of *Beowulf* have continued apace, and basic reference works and studies of the *Beowulf* manuscript that facilitate work on style and theme have appeared. Probably the most important of the works dealing directly with style and theme are two books by Andy Orchard, *A Critical Companion to* Beowulf (Cambridge: D. S. Brewer, 2003), and *Pride and Prodigies: Studies in the Monsters of the* Beowulf *Manuscript* (University of Toronto Press, 1995). Throughout *A Critical Companion to Beowulf* Orchard gives scrupulous attention to the poet's artful deployment of apposition, wordplay, rhyme, significant parallels, and envelope patterns in the poem and scrutinizes carefully the poet's ultimate purpose. He gives a balanced assessment of the Christian and traditional pre-Christian material in the poem. Starting with the poet's reference (in his own voice) to Cain, Abel, and the Flood, Orchard provides a comprehensive account of every place in the poem where a statement or image can be paralleled in a Christian text (hagiographical, homiletic, patristic, etc.). Only some of these parallels would have been detected by an audience hearing or reading the poem, I suspect, and those occurring in the speech or actions of pagan characters would function primarily to impart a vague aura of Christian rectitude to those characters. The parallels would not, I believe, have been perceived as specific allusions to Christian texts but rather would give the audience a reassuring sense that their pagan ancestors were capable at times of speaking and acting in ways that were consonant with the ethics and ideals of Christianity. The parallels cannot alter the heathen characters' destiny, but they can give them dignity in the esteem of a Christian audience.

Orchard gives an illuminating account of the speeches in the poem (fully 38 percent of the total text, according to his estimate) and clarifies the role of Unferth, Wiglaf, and other characters as expressed in their speeches. He detects in Wiglaf's discourse negative assessments of the hero that I do not see. Beowulf, it seems to me, is in every way an ideal protagonist in his pagan context and tragically deficient only from the poet's Christian perspective.

Orchard's footnotes, it should be noted, display an almost awesome command of scholarship and literary sources relevant to *Beowulf* and also many shrewd textual criticisms of specific passages in the poem.

In *Pride and Prodigies* Orchard situates *Beowulf* in the context of other texts in the *Beowulf* manuscript (the Nowell codex) and in relation to the *Liber Monstrorum* and the Old Norse *Grettis* saga, two texts that have long been associated with *Beowulf.* He argues convincingly that all these texts extol the heroic glory of a pagan age viewed from the perspective of a Christian people who acknowledge that pagan glory was nonetheless unavailing in a Christian context. Thus the theme of *Beowulf* as it is described in *Appositive Style* was a theme general to more than one literary text in the early middle ages of the Germanic people.

In the opening chapter of *Appositive Style* it is suggested that "the poet of *Beowulf* attempts to build a place in his people's collective memory for their lost ancestors" (13). This overarching memorial function of the poem has now received expansive and detailed treatment in Matthias Eitelmann's *Beowulfes Beorh: Das altenglische 'Beowulf'-Epos als kultureller Gedächtnisspeicher* (Heidelberg: Universitätsverlag Winter, 2010). In characterizing the poem as primarily a storehouse of cultural memory Eitelmann confirms conclusively this important dimension of *Beowulf* and explains well the place the poem so conceived holds in early medieval literature at large. The book is rich with other themes as well. The author gives a resourceful account of Beowulf's demeanor at his reception in Heorot, explaining it as an exercise in diplomacy, and he expands brilliantly on another theme in *Appositive Style,* "the conflict between anarchic nature and the world of human order." He points to an effective contrast between Grendel's implicit rejection of wergild and Hrothgar's compensation for

Hondscio—a telling demonstration of the restoration of human order after the monster's lawless anarchism. Throughout his book Eitelmann also brings to his readings relevant elements of postmodern theory, connections unattempted in *Appositive Style*.

Christine Rauer in *Beowulf and the Dragon: Parallels and Analogues* (D. S. Brewer, 2000) convincingly places *Beowulf* in the context of hagiographical accounts of saints battling dragons, noting that "the poet may have used religious source material for emphatically secular contexts of *Beowulf*" (142). Her conception of the poet's "syncretic mode of composition" (136) needs to be taken into account in considering any overall interpretation of the poem, such as that in *Appositive Style*.

In *Language, Sign, and Gender in* Beowulf (Carbondale: Southern Illinois University Press, 1990) Gillian R. Overing extends persuasively our sense of the openness of the poem's style and language. A close scrutiny of "the process of meaning construction from within and without the poem" shows how *Beowulf* eludes resolution and finality, leaving us with an open-ended text. A perceptive analysis of the poet's presentation of three women—Wealhtheow, Hildeburh, and Modthryth—illustrates how the poem rests largely with paradox and ambiguity.

A valuable contribution is Charles Dahlberg's application of appositive style to an analysis of kingship in the poem in his *The Literature of Unlikeness* (Hanover, NH: University Press of New England, 1988), 42–54.

John M. Hill, *The Cultural World in* Beowulf (Toronto: University of Toronto Press, 1993), 49–55, gives a thoughtful (and critical) assessment of the argument in *Appositive Style*.

Nida Lousie Surber-Meyer traces learnedly the motifs of ritual and artifact in the scenes of gift-giving and exchange in the poem in her *Gift and Exchange in the Anglo-Saxon Poetic Corpus* (Geneva: Editions Slatkine, 1994), 88, 141, et passim.

Some studies have applied elements of *Appositive Style* to the analysis of literatures other than Old English. The best of these is Roderick Walter McTurk's "The Poetic Edda and the Appositive Style," *Atti del 12° Congresso Internationale di Studi sull'alto medioevo* (Spoleto, 1990), 321–37. McTurk clarifies and refines the varieties of apposition (he prefers the term "variation") in the

Old Norse Edda and also adds clarification to some of the examples cited in *Appositive Style*.

Works of reference and more general studies of Beowulf that can contribute to further study of the style and theme of the poem have appeared in abundance since the publication of *Appositive Style*. The only comprehensive bibliography of writings on *Beowulf* available when *Appositive Style* was being written was Douglas D. Short's Beowulf *Scholarship: An Annotated Bibliography* (New York: Garland, 1980), which dealt with publications only through the year 1978. Robert J. Hasenfratz's Beowulf *Scholarship: An Annotated Bibliography, 1979–1990* (Garland, 1993) provides an excellent account of publications during the following eleven years. For those who prefer printed sources to online information these bibliographies (with excellent summaries of each item included) updated by the annual bibliographies in the *Old English Newsletter* provide a full record of scholarship and criticism.

A reliable and very accessible introduction to the poem, Marijane Osborn's *Beowulf: A Guide to Study* (Eugene, OR: Wipf and Stock, 2004), gives readers an excellent start in the study of style and theme, with chapters on the plot and subplot of the poem, the pagan-Christian question, structure and style. If one prefers online access, there is Roy M. Liuzza's "*Beowulf*: A Study Guide" web. utk.edu/~rliuzza/Beowulf/. For an intelligent selection of essays on many aspects of the poem see *Beowulf: Basic Readings*, ed. Peter S. Baker (New York: Garland, 1995), and for valuable insights on style and theme see Daniel Donoghue, *Old English Literature: A Short Introduction* (Malden, MA: Blackwell, 2004), 23–40.

Two editions which bear significantly on the style and theme of *Beowulf* are *Beowulf: an Edition with Relevant Shorter Texts*, edited by Bruce Mitchell and Fred C. Robinson (Oxford: Blackwell, 1998, revised with corrections, 2006) and *Klaeber's "Beowulf" and "The Fight at Finnsburg,"* fourth edition, revised by R. D. Fulk, Robert E. Bjork, and John D. Niles (Toronto: University of Toronto Press, 2008). The former is especially suitable for classroom use; the latter is valuable for its comprehensive account of the scholarship on the poem. Both editions have a great deal to say about style and theme.

Important improvements in access to the Beowulf manuscript have been made since the publication of Appositive Style. The British Academy has put on line an electronic version of MS Cotton Vitellius A.xv (The *Beowulf* manuscript): http://www.bl.uk/manuscripts/FullDisplay.aspx?ref=Cotton_MS_vitellius_a_xv. An electronic edition of the manuscript by Kevin Kiernan makes available the many manuscript readings which have been covered in the process of preserving the manuscript, readings not available in the British Library version. For information go to the *Electronic Beowulf* website: http://ebeowulf.uky.edu/studyingbeo wulfs/criticaledition#backlitimages. The same section of Kiernan's critical edition concisely explains how readers can instantly access any Thorkelin A or B transcript of words in the manuscript, these being two copies of the *Beowulf* manuscript made in the eighteenth century, copies which record manuscript readings subsequently lost. Meanwhile, J. R. Hall is recovering all the readings attested by scholars who have made transcripts of the manuscript in the eighteenth and nineteenth centuries; some of the recovered readings have already been published and all of them will appear soon in book form. See J. R. Hall, "Supplementary Evidence and the Manuscript Text of *Beowulf*: A Survey of Sources," *English Past and Present: Selected Papers from the IAUPE Conference in 2010,* ed. Wolfgang Viereck (Frankfurt am Main: Peter Lang, 2012), 9–25.

Representative of the work that has been done on the meter of *Beowulf* since 1985 is Geoffrey Russom's Beowulf *and Old Germanic Metre* (Cambridge: Cambridge University Press, 1998).

Of translations of the poem made since 1985 three bear special mention. R. M. Liuzza, Beowulf: *A New Verse Translation* (Peterborough, Ont., Orchard Park, NY: Broadview Press, 2000), offers a faithful yet readable verse translation and excellent notes and commentary, which are very helpful to students coming to the poem for the first time. Daniel Donoghue, editor, and Seamus Heaney, translator, *Beowulf: A Verse Translation* (New York: Norton, 2002), contains a fine verse translation by the Nobel laureate. *Beowulf and Other Old English Poems,* edited and translated by Craig Williamson (Philadelphia: University of Pennsylvania Press, 2002) is valuable both for its translation and its extensive commentary. Useful discussions of translation and other aspects of the poem are in *Beowulf at Kalamazoo: Essays on Translation and Performance*, edited by Jana K. Schulman and Paul E. Szarmach (Kalamazoo: Medieval Institute Publications, 2012).

Textual criticism of discrete passages in the poem often bear directly on matters of theme and style. Such discussions are by various scholars and are published in a variety of places too numerous to cite in detail here. Some of the most important contributions on the text of *Beowulf* by the brilliant textual critic Alfred Bammesberger are collected in his *Linguistic Notes on Old English Poetic Texts* (Heidelberg: Carl Winter, 1986), 75–104.

Finally a comprehensive coverage of all aspects of the poem is *A Beowulf Handbook,* edited by Robert E. Bjork and John D. Niles (Lincoln: University of Nebraska Press, 1997).

These publications and others too numerous to mention all provide a solid foundation for further study of the topics dealt with in *Appositive Style*.

PREFACE

When the following chapters were presented as the John C. Hodges Lectures in Knoxville in 1982, they bore the title "Dark Age Heroism and Christian Regret: The Appositive Art of *Beowulf.*" I have preferred the present title as a more economical description of the content of the lectures, and yet in one respect the original version was superior: it emphasized that my concern is as much with the subject as with the style of *Beowulf.* My attempt to describe the workings of the "appositive" style is motivated by the conviction that this was for the poet an enabling style, the only style by which he could communicate his Christian vision of pagan heroic life "in geardagum." Central to that style is the loose, paratactic quality typified by the pervasive grammatical appositions of Old English poetry. These chapters examine apposition (or "variation," as it is often called by scholars of Germanic poetry) as well as poetic compounds, amphibolies, and certain narrative devices, all of which, like apposition, are suggestive and open rather than unambiguously assertive, all being in some sense equivocal. The controlled equivocations of the appositive style condition the audience's mind, in turn, to be receptive to the most important of the poet's expressive devices, his use of apposed meanings of words which had been given simultaneous Christian and pre-Christian senses by the Cædmonian renovation of Old English poetic diction. This device, reinforced constantly by all the other elements of appositive style, seems to me to afford the poet a means of resolving the Christian-pagan tension which pervades his narration of ancient heroic deeds.

The three chapters proceed in a way more circular than linear. The first describes the poem's major theme as I understand it and describes the poet's appositive strategies at both narrow grammatical and broad stylistic levels. The second chapter is primarily concerned with the poet's use of the semantically stratified vocabulary of

Old English poetry to accommodate a dual perspective on the events narrated, partly Christian and partly pre-Christian. The final chapter returns to the appositional techniques used in the poem and seeks to show that, in addition to serving the poet's major themes, these work in a variety of ways to implement his narrative purposes. This effort to reaffirm the fundamental role of appositive style in the poem also results in new ways of reading some familiar passages in *Beowulf.*

Although my focus throughout is on theme and style, I have found it necessary to advert repeatedly to another favorite subject of mine which I believe to be worthy of attention in and of itself. Modern editors and lexicographers who mediate between the poem in its manuscript state and the modern reader all too often obscure important stylistic effects when they modernize the format of the text. Often and unconsciously readers have had their interpretations of the poem restricted or even predetermined by glossaries and dictionaries which arbitrarily disambiguate the grammar of nominal compounds and the meanings of polysemous words, by modern conventions of punctuation which (as Bruce Mitchell has recently shown) limit the multiple reference of Old English syntactical constructions, and by modern conventions of capitalization which interfere with the poet's subtle strategy in presenting the pre-Christian heroes' spiritual status. By sharpening our awareness of these inadvertent editorial obfuscations, we may come closer to recovering the poem which the *Beowulf* poet bequeathed to us.

ACKNOWLEDGMENTS

I owe heartfelt thanks to John H. Fisher, Carol Orr, Mary Richards, and Joseph B. Trahern, Jr., of the University of Tennessee for getting me started on this study and then for waiting with saintly patience for me to finish it. For various kinds of encouragement and enlightenment I am grateful to Larry D. Benson, Morton Bloomfield, and Jan Ziolkowski of Harvard University, to Thomas D. Hill of Cornell University, and to Merja Kytö of the University of Helsinki.

Beowulf and the Appositive Style

1. APPOSITIVE STYLE
AND THE THEME OF *BEOWULF*

A recent edition of John C. Hodges's *Harbrace College Handbook* defines "appositive" as "a noun or noun substitute set beside another noun or noun substitute and identifying or explaining it."[1] Thus in the sentence "the hero of the poem is Beowulf, king of the Geatas," "Beowulf" and "king of the Geatas" are in apposition, since they stand next to one another, have no word connecting them, and have the same referent, one element explaining or identifying the other. Etymologically *The Harbrace College Handbook* is correct in saying that an appositive is "set beside" another noun, for the Latin *appositus* means "placed (next) to." But in practice appositives can sometimes be separated from the word to which they refer, as in "Beowulf was there, the king of the Geatas." Also, some grammarians extend the meaning of "appositive" to include parts of speech other than the noun and to include even phrases and clauses.[2] What is essential, apparently, is that the two elements in an appositive construction be the same part of speech, have the same referent, and not be connected except by syntactical parallelism within the sentence in which they occur. "Appositive" in this broad sense describes fairly accurately what Anglo-Saxon scholars term "variation" in Old English poetry. "Variation" has been defined as "syntactically parallel words or word-groups which share a common referent and which occur within a single clause."[3] A ubiquitous feature in Old Germanic poetry, variation is, according to Frederick Klaeber, "the very soul of the Old English poetical style."[4]

The distinguishing feature of apposition (or variation) is its parataxis—its lack of an expressed logical connection between the apposed elements. "Beowulf, king of the Geatas" is apposition; "Beowulf was king of the Geatas" is not. The relationship between the elements of an appositive construction and the relevance of these

elements to the sentence at large must be inferred from their proxi-
mate and parallel status. In Old English poetry, where apposition is
used so heavily, the construction often seems especially rich in implicit meaning, as the following examples from *Beowulf* may suggest.

> Nealles him on heape   handgesteallan,
> æðelinga bearn   ymbe gestodon   [2596–97]

"The comrades, the sons of noblemen, did not stand by him together
at all." Only so much is overtly stated about the cowardly retainers
who abandoned Beowulf in his time of need. But implicit are the
logical relationships among the apposed elements: "Although sons
of noblemen and thus especially obligated to stand firm at the hand
of the leader, they did not stand by him together at all." This
rendition of the poet's logically reticent paratactic sentence into an
elaborately explicit hypotactic version is not entirely arbitrary; it is, I
believe, implied in the selection of the two terms in apposition and
especially by the implied relationship between the components of the
compound *handgesteallan*.[5] Similarly implicit relationships may be
suspected in Wiglaf's appositions in his rueful comment about the
Geatas' efforts to dissuade Beowulf from facing the dragon:

> Ne meahton we gelæran   leofne þeoden,
> rices hyrde   ræd ænigne,
> þæt he ne grette   goldweard þone

"We could not persuade the dear prince, the guardian of the kingdom, that he should leave the dragon unchallenged." The appositives
"leofne þeoden" and "rices hyrde" seem to supply the respective
motivations of the persuading subjects and the unpersuaded king:
"Because the prince was beloved to us, we begged him not to fight the
dragon, but since he was a conscientious guardian of his kingdom, he
insisted on doing so." The poet says only that Beowulf was a prince
beloved by his subjects and a guardian of his kingdom; he leaves to
inference the relevance these juxtaposed descriptive phrases have in
their context.

Occasionally, when a character in the poem wishes to suggest
logical relationships without overtly stating them, this suggestive
power of apposition becomes a part of the dramatic action. In his
farewell speech to Hrothgar, Beowulf wishes to assure the Danish
king that the Geatas stand ready to help him in the event of either
attack from without or treachery from within. If foreign armies

resume hostilities, declares Beowulf, he will bring to Hrothgar's defense "a forest of spears, the support of an army."[6] Turning to the other source of danger, the incipient power struggle at which Wealhtheow has persistently hinted,[7] Beowulf dares not speak so openly. In order to convey his meaning without declaring it in the full hearing of Hrothulf and the other Danes, he resorts to an implicitly significant apposition:

> Gif him þonne Hreþric   to hofum Geata
> geþingeð þeodnes bearn,   he mæg þær fela
> freonda findan   [1836–38]

This has usually been taken as merely a polite invitation: if Hrethric should come to Geatland, he will find friends there. But the appositive "þeodnes bearn" subtly calls attention to Hrethric's standing in the line of succession to the Danish throne: he is the eldest son of Hrothgar. Wealhtheow's anxious allusions to her sons' succession and her appeals to Beowulf to support them (1178–87, 1219–20, 1226–27) give special significance to this seemingly casual appositive. Moreover, Beowulf describes Hrethric's visit with the curious expression "him . . . geþingeð [MS geþinged]," implying arrangements or negotiations rather than a casual visit,[8] while the cryptic maxim with which Beowulf concludes the speech ("feorcyþðe beoð / selran gesohte þæm þe him selfa deah") seems to hint at more serious purposes than a pleasure trip. The unique compound *feorcyþðu* could mean "close friends who are afar" (i.e., distant allies) as well as the usually assumed "far countries" and would then refer to the same people as *freonda* in the first half of the verse. Beowulf's carefully phrased advice and veiled assurances prompt Hrothgar to sudden and enthusiastic praise of his wisdom and his skill at speech. (He praises Beowulf's *wordcwydas* twice in five lines: 1841–45.) If my reading is correct, then this passage depicts a character in the poem using an appositive phrase with subtle significance and another character reacting to that use. If the poet has his characters use apposition with calculated effect, then it should not seem oversubtle to see such effects in his own use of the construction when he is speaking in his own voice.

As we shall soon see, the logically open, implicit quality of apposition is shared by other stylistic devices in the poem, and in concert these create a reticent, appositive style which is intimately cooperative with the tone and theme of the poem. Before we turn to these other appositive devices, however, we should perhaps address the question of the theme of *Beowulf,* since after doing so we shall find it easier to relate the stylistic devices to that theme.

What is the theme of *Beowulf?* There will never be universal agreement on this question, and yet there is considerable common ground among critics of the poem, especially those who, like me, start from a general acceptance of the landmark essay by J.R.R. Tolkien, *"Beowulf:* The Monsters and the Critics."[9] Central to this Tolkienian view of the poem is the contrast between the time and milieu of the poet and the time and milieu of the characters in his poem. Like most heroic poems of Western culture—the *Iliad* and *Odyssey,* the *Aeneid,* the *Song of Roland,* the *Nibelungenlied*[10]— *Beowulf* is about a bygone era. The action of the poem is set in the fifth and sixth centuries, and the people it describes are remote pagan ancestors of the Anglo-Saxons, living on the continent of Europe in and near the lands whence the English migrated to the British Isles and, after many generations, became Christians. The events recounted conform in outline and in some detail with what we know of the history of pagan Germania, and yet the time and the setting are sufficiently distant that monsters and dragons can assume a place in the narrative without disturbing the verisimilitude of the more historical elements, partly, no doubt, because everything in the poem is felt to have taken place in a far lost, primordial past.

Exactly how much time elapsed between the action of *Beowulf* and the time of the poet and his audience depends upon the exact date of the poem's composition. Until recently there was a broad scholarly consensus that *Beowulf* reached more or less its present form sometime in the eighth century. In the wake of Ashley Crandell Amos's crucially important reassessment of linguistic methods of dating Old English texts, however, a series of radical reappraisals of the bases for dating the poem have now reopened the question of date in an almost dismaying fashion.[11] Some authorities stubbornly cling to the conviction that the poem was composed in the eighth century, while others (most prominently Kevin Kiernan) argue that the poem could not have been written before A.D. 1016. And there are arguments for various dates between these extremes. I am inclined to favor an earlier rather than a later date. The alliteration of palatal and velar *g*, which Amos confirms is still a valid criterion of early poetry,[12] implies a date probably before the early to mid tenth century, when the allophones of *g* began to be perceived by poets as two distinct sounds. Moreover, while it is true that scholars have demolished the old argument that *Beowulf* could not have been composed after the period of Scandinavian invasions and settlement,[13] I do not believe the case is strong for a post-invasion *Beowulf* poet's having taken his story from contemporary Scandinavian sources. The forms of the proper names in the Old English poem bear no traces of transmission through ninth- or tenth-century Norse, and the stories in *Beowulf* and the manner of their telling do not closely resemble surviving Norse poetry. But these arguments are not probative, and when such learned and formidable challenges to an early date have been posed, minds must remain open. Whatever the poem's date, everyone will agree that there is a chasm of time— two to four centuries—separating the poet from the dramatic action of his poem, and during that time there was a transforming migration, both geographical and theological. Few readers would deny that *Beowulf* is a profoundly retrospective narrative.

Why does the poet reach back so far in time for his subject matter? Why does a person living in a settled realm, with church and coinage and law codes to help order his existence and written documents to protect his interests and enrich his mind—why should such a person compose a poem about barely literate tribes striving for fame and hegemony in the ancient Germanic lands of the north? The poet's life was far different from that of his characters, not least because he and his contemporaries were Christian, with a rich Christian literature to comfort them and a clear Christian formula to explain the hopeless plight of their heathen ancestors, while the characters in the poem are these very heathen ancestors, living in a benighted and violent world. They were deprived of the revelation which offered the poet and his audience escape from the damnation which awaits all heathens, including, apparently, the heroes of *Beowulf.*

In the poet's Christian world there was no uncertainty as to the nature of heathenism as contrasted with that of Christianity. Christianity is the Truth. Paganism is a network of deceptions and lies fabricated by the Devil to ensnare the ignorant. Through Christianity a person can find salvation. Without Christianity, according to the voices that spoke for the Church, a person is lost eternally. The three damnatory clauses distributed throughout the Athanasian Creed reiterate ominously the sure perdition which awaits those who have not heard and accepted the articles of the faith.[14] Mark 16:16 gives powerful scriptural support to this view,[15] as do Church Fathers such as St. Cyprian, who insisted quite simply that "there is no salvation outside the Church." In his letter describing the pagan Saxons as being "of one blood and one bone" with the Christian English, St. Boniface makes it clear that without conversion these Germanic brethren were forever lost to the Devil.[16]

English kings who traced their lineage back to Woden, and English aristocrats who took pride in the works and wisdom of their continental forebears, had, then, to acknowledge upon becoming Christians that their ancestors were consigned to eternal damnation. More than that, the Christian mentors of the Anglo-Saxons demanded that the ancestors be consigned to oblivion as well. Alcuin's frequently cited letter to the monks of Lindisfarne remains the locus classicus for this view: "Let the words of God be read at the meal of the clergy. There it is proper to listen to the lector, not a harp-player; the sermons of the Fathers, not songs of the people. For what has Ingeld to do with Christ? Narrow is the house; it cannot hold both. The King of Heaven wants nothing to do with so-called kings who are pagan and damned. For the eternal King reigns in heaven; the damned pagan laments in hell."[17] Some critics have felt that too much has been made of this passage, arguing that Alcuin speaks only for himself when he exhorts the monks at Lindisfarne. But in fact Alcuin's statement about the importance of divorcing oneself utterly from the traditions of non-Christians is merely an adaptation of a widely expressed medieval Christian doctrine. In Corinthians II, 6:14–15, St. Paul provides the biblical paradigm for this tenet: "Be ye not unequally yoked together with unbelievers: for what fellowship hath righteousness with unrighteousness? and what communion hath light with darkness? and what concord hath Christ with Belial, or what part hath he that believeth with an infidel?" Among the Church Fathers who repeated this injunction is Tertullian, who seems almost obsessed with it. In *De spectaculis*, chapters 26–27, he condemns those who listen to a tragedian at heathen assemblies with the challenge "What fellowship has light with darkness, life with death?" Elsewhere he reiterates the antithesis in various forms: "What has Athens to do with Jerusalem?" "What communion has Christ with Belial?" "What part has a believer with an infidel?" "What commerce have the condemners with those who are condemned? The same, I assume, as Christ with Belial."[18] St. Jerome adopts Tertullian's antithesis, adding the query, "What has Horace to do with the Psalter?"[19] Pope Zacharias in a letter to St. Boniface had also used the antithesis, and the eighth-century biographer of St. Eligius asks what use there could be for the nonsense of Homer and Virgil or the writings of heathens like Sallust and Herodotus.[20] The phrasing of the question in the *Gemma animae* seems to owe something to Alcuin: "Of what benefit to the soul are the battles of Hector or the disputations of Plato or the poems of Virgil or the songs of Ovid, all of whom are wailing with their ilk in the prison of the infernal Babylon under the grim rule of Pluto?" *(PL* CLXXII, cols. 543–44). The exhortation to Christians to reject the pre-Christian past—whether Hector or Horace or Athens or Ingeld—is in no sense, then, an aberration of Alcuin's. It is a serious Christian belief grafted deeply into Anglo-Saxon thought, but with reference to Germanic rather than to Classical paganism. The proscription continues into the later Anglo-Saxon period, with Ælfric instructing his fellow priests, "Forbeode ge þa hæðenan sangas þæra læwedra manna," and Wulfstan proclaiming, "And we læraƌ þæt man geswice freolsdagum hæþenra leoƌa and deofles gamena."[21]

And yet it is precisely the condemned, pre-Christian past to which the *Beowulf* poet devotes his poem. Though a Christian addressing Christians, he does not treat the Christian heroes celebrated by so many of his fellow poets but turns his gaze instead back to the dark and hopeless epoch and recreates for his own age the times and people whom the churchmen wanted forgotten. He cannot pretend these people were Christian, nor can he just quietly ignore their desperate spiritual state, as some modern critics have wanted to believe. From the very beginning, when the poem is set temporally "in geardagum" and geographically "Scedelandum in," the audience would assume that the subject of the narrative is pre-Christian Germanic folk, and when they hear the names of Scyld Scefing, Beowulf, Healfdene, Hrothgar, Heorogar, and Halga in swift succession, names familiar to them from other poems and from genealogies, their assumption would have been confirmed. The impressive funeral of Scyld would have seemed the appropriate rite for this pagan people, and their bewilderment at the attacks by Grendel would have been expected, since they (unlike the audience) had no knowledge of his descent from Cain. Noting these clear signs of a pagan setting, the audience would have felt less surprise, I believe, than most modern readers seem to feel at the poet's account in 175–88 of the Scyldings' worship at pagan shrines, vow to make sacrifices to their demon gods, and ignorant commission of their souls to hell by their tragically misguided piety. The reason modern readers have been surprised by the "pagan excursus" and have even wanted to excise this passage as a later interpolation is, I believe, that they have not been sufficiently aware of just how persistently the poet has included details of heathen life in *Beowulf*, both before the pagan excursus and throughout the ensuing poem. It may be well to review some of these details and then to suggest why they have seemed inconspicuous to most readers.

The cremations which are described or are alluded to in 1107–24, 2126, 2802–8, 2818, 3097, and 3110–80 would themselves assure that the audience could not lose sight of the paganism of the poem's characters.[22] The references to burying treasure or other grave goods with the dead would also have identified the Danes and Geatas as non-Christian,[23] and indeed the buried treasure of the dragon's hoard is specifically called "hæðen gold" and "hæðen hord" in 2216 and 2276. Reading omens of various kinds to divine the future or to determine the best times for traveling is regularly condemned in laws, sermons, and other writings of the period,[24] and so when the Geatas are introduced to us in the act of reading the omens before Beowulf's embarking for Denmark, their theological status is made clear. When the scene of the poem shifts to Geatland, the poet again specifies the Geatas' paganism, if we agree with Håkan Ringbom that the original manuscript reading *hæðnum,* "heathens" (with *ð* erased), should displace the editors' emendations in 1983.[25] Such an emphatic reaffirmation of their heathenism here would be interesting but not necessary, since their pre-Christian status is made clear generally, if more subtly, elsewhere in the poem. The allusion to totemic animals (boar, hart, and "snake swords")[26] in the context of other pagan practices would likely have assumed heathen associations, and Beowulf's speeches about the preferability of blood vengeance to mourning and about the importance of fame after death would certainly have carried such connotations.

Given the frequency and repetition of such pagan details throughout the poem, we might well ask why readers have so often overlooked them and have tried to imagine a Christian setting for the poem or a setting devoid of any religious coloration at all. One reason is that the poet has by design selected the more inconspicuous, inoffensive tokens of heathenism for iteration throughout *Beowulf* because he does not wish his audience to lose sympathy with the poem's characters. He wants them to accept the heathenism of the men of old and to join him in regretting it, but then he wishes to take his audience beyond this recognition of their spiritual status to a sympathetic evaluation of them for what they were. He does not show his heroes exposing children, performing human sacrifice,[27] or practicing witchcraft, and except for the one description of the Danes' idol worship (175–78), we are not made to see them at their pagan rites. He avoids calling the pagan gods by name,[28] and he even uses terms like *hæðen* somewhat sparingly,[29] in order that his portrayal of his characters will not repel the very audience whose sympathetic hearing he wants to engage. Another reason why readers have tended to pass over the mild yet pervasive signs of paganism in Beowulfian society is that the pagan characters use pious expressions and Christian-sounding allusions which have given some people the impression that Beowulf, Hrothgar, and other characters in the poem are in fact Christians, despite the anachronistic absurdity of such an assumption. This problem is the subject of my second chapter, where I shall try to show that the pseudo-Christian language used by characters in the poem is, like the inconspicuous pagan details, a calculated effect of the poet's and, indeed, perhaps his greatest achievement in adapting his pagan heroes for a devoutly Christian audience in such a way that the audience can admire those heroes while remaining fully aware of their hopeless paganism.

It will be argued throughout this study that a combined admiration and regret is the dominant tone in *Beowulf* and that one of the poet's signal triumphs was to adopt the precisely appropriate style for striking that tone. Admiration for pagans, however, has often been judged a highly improbable attitude for medieval Christians to assume. Many readers have held that moral revulsion is the only possible reaction that a converted Anglo-Saxon could have when confronted with pagans. But Larry D. Benson has skillfully demonstrated that this is not the case.[30] Citing, among other sources, the letters of St. Boniface, Benson shows that Anglo-Saxons often reacted to the paganism of their continental cousins compassionately and with "intense sympathy for their plight" (p. 201). The description of the Danes' heathenism in *Beowulf*, Benson notes, emphasizes the blameless ignorance of the idol worshipers, who are "ensnared in devilish errors through no fault of their own." This view seems to be supported by a text which was published after "The Pagan Coloring of *Beowulf*" was in print. In his sermon *De falsis diis*, Ælfric describes how the Devil first induced people to euhemerize famous men and build idols to them and then entered those idols and spoke through them deceptively to the worshipers, whose souls were thus betrayed into hell's punishment. Ælfric's attitudes call to mind the passage in *Beowulf:* "Þa gesawon þa deoflu, þe hi beswicon on ær, / þa fægran anlicnyssa, and flugon þarto, / and þurh þa anlic-nyssa spræcon to þam earmum mannum, / and hi swa forlæddon mid heora leasungum, / and to hellicum suslum heora sawla gebrohtan."[31] Here as in *Beowulf* the Devil is blamed and the heathens are pitied: the demons "spoke through the idols to those poor people and misled them with their deceptions and brought their souls to the torments of hell." If even so stern a Christian as Ælfric could join in this compassionate attitude toward benighted, idol-worshiping pagans, there seems little reason to doubt that *Beowulf*, Boniface, and other sources cited by Benson could, at an earlier time, have reflected a similar attitude. The virtues of the Beowulfian heroes are extolled and are even held up as models for behavior in the poet's own day ("Swa sceal mæg don," "Swa sceal geong guma," "Swa sceal man don"), while at the same time the poet never loses sight of the hard fact that these are pagans, and pagans, say the churchmen, are damned.

Not every medieval Christian, it is true, was content to consign all virtuous pagans to hell. Dante's sadness about Virgil's status in the afterlife, and his apparent view that the righteous pagan Ripheus gained entry into Heaven (*Paradiso* XX, 122–24), bear witness to his agonized concern for the fate of the good heathen.[32] In at least one version of Jacobus de Voragine's *Legenda aurea,* Trajan seems to have gained salvation through the prayers of Gregory, although there is considerable disagreement about the conditions and even the possibility of Trajan's salvation.[33] Later, the problem of the virtuous heathen is raised in *Piers Plowman.*[34] It is hardly surprising, then, that, as early as the Anglo-Saxon period, some thinkers may have been looking for ways to save the virtuous heathen. Charles Donahue's articles on Irish speculations as to how good heathens might gain entry to Heaven show that the stern Augustinian attitude toward heathens was not the only one possible among Christians,[35] and the persistence of the Pelagian heresy in the British Isles would suggest some discomfort with the notion that every unbaptized soul was damned. But as Benson has well demonstrated, the central tradition was in accord with the views of St. Augustine, Bede, Boniface, and other churchmen who agreed that salvation without conversion was impossible.[36] If the *Beowulf* poet knew about a softer theological position on the heathen, he did not appeal to it in his poem. It is true, as Morton Bloomfield has noted, that there is an implicit parallel between the pre-Mosaic patriarchs of the Old Testament and the Beowulfian characters, since both lived without knowledge of either the Old Law or the New.[37] But while this parallel may give the Christian English room for a certain pride of ancestry, it does not grant salvation. For all the *Beowulf* poet says, we are left with heroes who are pathetic in their heathenism while being at the same time noble in their thoughts and actions; they are exemplary but cannot save themselves. Statius says to Virgil (*Purgatorio* XXII, 67–73), "You were like one who goes by night and carries the light behind him and profits not himself, but makes those wise who follow him,"[38] and a Christian Anglo-Saxon might say the same to Beowulf.

From this complex attitude toward his subject, the poet of *Beowulf* attempts to build a place in his people's collective memory for their lost ancestors. This lofty and challenging theme requires for its expression an appositive style, a style more suggestive than assertive, more oblique than direct. A poet who, in a deeply Christian age, wants to acknowledge his heroes' damnation while insisting on their dignity must find and exercise in his listeners' minds the powers of inference and the ability to entertain two simultaneous points of view that are necessary for the resolution of poignant cultural tensions. As we turn now to a systematic examination of the elements of appositive style, we shall see that common to them all is this quality of implicitness or logical openness. Not every ambiguity or deliberate indeterminacy is directly related to the paradoxical portrayal of the poem's characters as people to be both admired and regretted, but each such effect makes its contribution toward the creation of a general atmosphere in the poem where such a complex attitude toward a people can be made both understandable and comforting to an Anglo-Saxon audience.

We have already given attention to some of the inferential demands made by grammatical apposition. Another basic element of the *Beowulf* poet's style which is juxtapositional in character and requires more inferences than is often noted is the compound, a cardinal feature of traditional Old English poetic diction.[39] That compounds are in a real sense appositional has been noted before.[40] Nominal compounds in particular seem to achieve their effect by a simple juxtaposing of independent elements, with the reader or audience being left to infer the relationship of the two and their composite meaning. Deducing the logical relationship between compound elements is not always as simple as we might expect. Thomas J. Gardner's study *Semantic Patterns in Old English Substantival Compounds* and Charles T. Carr's analysis of the semantic types of Germanic nominal compounds[41] show that the elements of a compound can stand in any one of various possible relationships with each other, and context must guide the reader or audience in electing the most appropriate one. Consider, for example, words like *deaðcwalu, deaðcwealm, freadrihten, gryreboga, gumman, modsefa, wældeað,* and *winedrihten* in *Beowulf.* In these compounds the two elements seem to refer more or less equally to the same referent. (This does not mean, of course, that the words are merely tautological; a *wældeað* is not the same as a death from natural causes, and a *winedrihten,* or lord and friend, is more than just a lord.) In other, seemingly similar compounds the first element appears to have a different, genitival relationship with the second: *gumdrihten* and *mondrihten* probably mean not "man and lord" (as we might assume from the pattern of *gumman,* "man-person") but rather "lord of men" (following the pattern of *folccyning* and *þeodcyning*). *Beorn-*

cyning, on the other hand, is ambiguous in syntactical structure. Some scholars take it to mean "hero-king," while others interpret it as "king of heroes." Ever since the first performance of *Beowulf*, readers or listeners have had to exercise their individual judgment as to how to construe this and many similar compounds.

The individual judgments forced upon the audience by the compounds in *Beowulf* constantly remind us of how syntactically open, how "appositional" the style of the poem is, especially if we free our minds of the false certainties with which modern glossaries beguile us. Klaeber's edition, for example, instructs us that *eorðcyning* means "king of the land," while *wyruldcyning* means "(earthly) king." But compounding being the open structure that it is, do not both words in fact mean both things, readers being forced to choose the more appropriate sense in any given context? Sometimes the poet uses the same compound in two separate contexts, one of which induces the reader to assign one kind of syntactic analysis and the other of which requires a different kind. When Heremod is exiled and punished by his nation, he is said to suffer *leodbealu*, "woe from his people" (*leod-* standing in a subjective-genitival relationship with *-bealu*); but when Modþryð (or Þryð)[42] curbs her behavior as a tyrannical and murderous queen, we are told that she inflicted less *leodbealu*—that is, less woe against her people (*leod-* standing here in an objective-genitival relationship with *-bealu*). Similarly, the nicor killed by the Geatas is said to have been separated from his swimming or his thrashing on the water (*yðgewinn*, 1434), but when we are told at 2412 that the dragon's hoard lay near the *yðgewinn* (which stands in apposition with *holmwylm*), we know that the elements of the compound must be related differently ("tumult of the waves," that is, "restless sea"), since no swimming takes place at this point. Depending on how we choose to analyze the compound *heofodweard* syntactically and semantically, the word can mean "bodyguard," "chapter," "chief protector," or "watch over the head." Klaeber's glossary definition "head-watch . . . (i.e., 'death-watch')" obscures from us the play of mind that the word required from an Anglo-Saxon audience, which had to exclude three common meanings before arriving at a fourth that satisfied the context. We may compare the effect that the word had on contemporary listeners or readers with the effect that "overrul'd" would have on readers of

Marlowe's *Hero and Leander* (167–68) in his own time or ours: "It lies not in our power to love or hate, / For will in us is *overrul'd* by fate." Context here forces the reader to exclude the common meaning "pronounce invalid" and adopt the more primitive sense "rule over, control." But the common meaning is faintly present, so that our experience of the sentence is slightly more complex than it would have been had Marlowe used a univocal word like "controlled" or "governed" rather than "overrul'd."

The variety of syntactic relationships that can exist between compound elements is further illustrated by the three compounds with the base word *-lufu* in *Beowulf: wiflufu, modlufu,* and *eardlufu.* Each of these entails a different syntactical relationship between its component elements: "love for a woman," "heart's love," and "beloved thing that is home, beloved home." The series *goldgyfa, goldmaððum,* and *goldwine* exhibits a similarly varied range of internal syntactical relationships. At times the syntactical structure of compounds remains unresolved in most readers' minds. Is a *wundorsmið* a smith who works by wondrous power or a smith who makes wondrous things? Is a *geosceaftgast* a creature serving fate's cruel purposes or a fated, doomed creature? Klaeber glosses *deaðscua* simply as "death-shadow," but what does that mean exactly—a deadly shadow, or the shadow of death, or a deadly thing that moves in darkness? In compounds like *meodustig* and *meoduwong,* the implicit relationship between the compound elements requires that the audience supply a good deal that is unexpressed: "path (to) the mead(-hall)," "plain (near) the mead(-hall)." These two words, like others discussed in this paragraph, are unique to *Beowulf,* as far as surviving records allow us to judge, and so the audience would probably have encountered them in few if any other contexts. It is likely, then, that the audience of *Beowulf* frequently had to infer the composite meaning of collocations which the listeners had rarely or never encountered before.

In emphasizing the syntactical openness of the poem's diction, I am not suggesting that the poet has no clearly defined meaning for the words he uses or that he is inviting us to impart to his poem whatever meaning we wish. Wherever the meanings of compounds are important (which is most of the time), context forces us to select one interpretation of the compound over other possible ones. *Mon-*

drihten in *Beowulf* almost certainly means "a lord who rules men" rather than "a lord who is a man"; *wiflufu* means "(a man's) love for a woman" rather than "a woman's love (for a man)," although in isolation from context all these meanings are possible. The difference between compounds and some other syntactical strategy for expressing relationships is not that the compound *in context* is less specifically meaningful but that part of the meaning is implicit rather than explicit, thus requiring of the reader more inferences and logical deductions than another linguistic form would demand.

One way of bringing into prominence the implicit quality of compounding is to imitate the method of some twentieth-century linguists for displaying the underlying structure and meaning of nominal compounds.[43] This method is based upon the assumption that compounds can best be regarded as reduced sentences or as transforms of complete sentences. Thus *wiflufu*, in its context in *Beowulf* 2065, implies a sentence "he lufað þæt wif"; underlying the two contrasting uses of *yðgewinn* in *Beowulf* 1434 and 2412 are the sentences "he winneð in þam yðum" and "þa yða winnað." The two possible interpretations of *beorncyning* remarked above can be expressed as "se cyning is beorn" and "se cyning wealdeð beornum."[44] Viewing the Beowulfian compounds in this way not only brings to light the variety of contrasting syntactical relationships latent in the juxtapositions which make up many compounds; it also reminds us of the wealth of verbal action which is implicit in the seemingly static nominalizations of Old English poetic diction. Indeed, in both nominal and adjectival compounds there are various kinds of verbal relationships implied (cf. *beadurun, hordwyrðe, lifbysig, nathwylc, sadolbeorht, sarigmod*), and if we add to the compounds the parallel system of forming nominal phrases—the noun-plus-genitival-noun collocations such as "yða gewinn" cf. *yðgewinn*, "gumena cynn" cf. *gumcynn*, "mægenes cræft" cf. *mægencræft*—we become aware that the often-remarked static quality of *Beowulf* is partly an illusion created by the chosen style. At the level of surface structure it is true that Old English verse is poetry of the noun and not of the verb, a grammatical propensity fostered in part by the accentual verse form. But beneath the surface, implicit in all these compounds and nominal phrases, the diction is alive with verbal activity. Both perspectives on the diction are important. At the level of meaning, the poet com-

17

municates all the verbal action and relationships his subject requires, but at the level of style he *seems* to avoid predications. This feature together with other elements of his paratactic style creates the impression of restraint and reticence in the poet's voice, a voice which seems often to supply facts without an accompanying interpretation of them. The syntactical ambiguities of compounds, which are so often overlooked by modern readers, make a modest and yet pervasive contribution to this restrained tone of the narrative.

As we have seen, one reason why modern readers tend to lose sight of the fundamentally ambiguous relation between the elements of nominal compounds is that glossaries and dictionaries systematically disambiguate these structures. At another level of expression, the modern punctuation which editors introduce into Old English texts serves a similar disambiguating function and further blinds readers to an underlying multiplicity of grammatical relationships which informs Old English poetic language. An important essay by Bruce Mitchell has recently called attention to ambiguous clause juncture in the syntax of the poetic language in general and of *Beowulf* in particular.[45] In a passage like *Beowulf* 1233–38 (here unpunctuated)

>   Wyrd ne cuþon
>   geosceaft grimme   swa hit agangen wearð
>   eorla manegum   syþðan æfen cwom
>   ond him Hroþgar gewat   to hofe sinum
>   rice to reste   reced weardode
>   unrim eorla   swa hie oft ær dydon

some editors punctuate so as to make the clause "syþðan . . . reste" dependent upon the preceding main clause and some upon the following. Mitchell argues that the *syþðan* clause more likely stands *apo koinou* and serves as a pivot between the two main clauses. At other times there is a syntactic openness in the very status of clauses, nothing in the original language indicating whether a clause is dependent or independent. But modern punctuation cannot tolerate such openness. Therefore, in passages like

>   se æt Heorote fand
>   wæccendne wer   wiges bidan
>   þær him aglæca   ætgræpe wearð   [1267–69]

and

hwilum heaþorofe   hleapan leton
on geflit faran   fealwe mearas
ðær him foldwegas   fægere þuhton
cystum cuðe   [864–67]

editors have variously interpreted the *þær* clauses as independent
("there the monster laid hold on him") or dependent ("where the
paths seemed pleasant to them"), with no apparent basis for their
decisions. In fact, it is only the rules of modern punctuation that force
a decision in the first place. The Old English sentences were probably
more fluid and structurally ambiguous, and the scribal practices of
the time preserved that fluidity. The numerous examples of such
openness which Mitchell sets out in his study (pp. 395–412) show
that the language was permeated by simultaneous reference of this
kind. The Anglo-Saxon audience, Mitchell implies, expected and
appreciated such amphibolies, while modern editors' punctuation is
constantly "eliminating options and blurring alternative connections and associations which were present in the poem created by the
poet" (p. 411). It is important to notice that Mitchell says not that the
syntax is uncontrolled but rather that it is capable of multiple reference and requires of the contemporary Anglo-Saxon audience that
same attention to syntactic relationships which we have already seen
to be requisite in the nominal compounds. "As in the structure of
compounds, so also in the structure of sentences much is left to the
sympathetic imagination of the hearer," observed Otto Jespersen
long ago,[46] and Mitchell's study shows that this is truer of Old
English than anyone had suspected as long as the punctuation of
modern editions blinded us to the actual genius of the language.

Another syntactic device which enlists the "sympathetic imagination of the hearer" of *Beowulf* is clausal apposition, the type of
construction which Walther Paetzel called *Satzvariationen* and
Gruppenvariationen (pp. 17–24). In clausal appositions phrases and
even entire independent clauses stand in the same relation to each
other as do individual words in simple appositions. Thus parallel
restatement of a verb and its object may occur (I italicize the apposed
elements):

ðy he *þone feond ofercwom*,
gehnægde helle gast   [1273–74]

19

ðonne *forstes bend* Fæder *onlæteð,*
onwindeð *wælrapas*   [1609–10]

The verb-object construction may include parallel instrumental nouns:

his freawine flane geswencte,
miste mercelses ond his mæg ofscet,
. . .   blodigan gare   [2438–40]

The parallel construction can consist of subject and predicate adjective:

                ða wæs Heregar dead,
min yldra mæg unlifigende   [467–68]

or of object and predicate adjective:

syðþan he aldorðegn   unlyfigendne,
þone deorestan deadne wisse   [1308–9]

or of entire independent clauses:

            Metod hie ne cuþon,
dæda Demend, ne wiston hie Drihten God [180–81]

Him þa ellenrof andswarode,
wlanc Wedera leod word æfter spræc [340–41][47]

ofer þæm hongiað hrinde bearwas,
wudu wyrtum fæst wæter oferhelmað [1363–64]

Besides illustrating the variety of types of clausal apposition in *Beowulf,* these examples show how these collocations, like the simple collocations discussed earlier in this chapter, are not merely tautological but rather supply various kinds of information if we reflect on the implications of the parallel structures. In the first example the initial predication "þone feond ofercwom" describes the victory from the hero's point of view, while the restatement "gehnægde helle gast" emphasizes the Christian narrator's ampler perspective on the vanquished monster. The poet in his own voice often specifies the hellish nature of the monsters, something of which the characters in the poem are unaware. In the second example the verbs give successive stages of the action, and the restated noun phrases develop the metaphor for frost. In the third, *freawine* and *mæg* bring out different aspects of the relationship between the two men—"lord and friend" and "kinsman"—while the words used to describe the arrow suggest progressive stages in the projectile's

course. *Flan* is alliteratively linked with words for "flight" so frequently in Old English that it probably suggested "arrow in flight."[48]
"Blodigan gare" presents the arrow after it has completed its flight
and has found its victim. The restatment "dead, unlifigende" seems
emotive, suggesting that the bereaved survivor was trying to come to
terms with a painful loss. (Cf. the apposition in Wordsworth's "No
motion has she now, no force.") "Aldorþegn unlyfigendne" also
involves a mournful quibble on *aldor-*, which means "life" as well as
"lord."

The poet's penchant for parallel statements which carry contrasting versions of the same action makes itself felt at times in simple
successions of sentences:

Beornas gearwe
on stefn stigon. . .
secgas bæron
on bearm nacan   beorhte frætwe,
guðsearo geatolic   [211–15]

Let ða of breostum,   ða he gebolgen wæs,
Weder-Geata leod   word ut faran,
stearcheort styrmde   [2550–52]

Swa se secg hwata   secggende wæs
laðra spella;   he ne leag fela
wyrda ne worda   [3028–30]

These are not clausal appositions in any strict sense, but the rhetoric
of such parallel clauses may have been influenced by the poet's
appositional propensity. Two statements relating to the same event
are juxtaposed without a connecting element. The reader is left to
infer whatever significance the juxtaposition may have. The third
example, with its characteristic collocation of a negative statement
following a positive one, is an instance of apposed sentences con-
veying an especially important implicit meaning: The messenger said
grievous things. The messenger said things that were not lies. In these
two sentences the poet validates the messenger's dire predictions,
informing us that the grim future foretold for the Geatas is indeed
imminent.

Not only are independent sentences juxtaposed with significant
effect; the poet at times extends this device to large segments of
narrative. A favorite means of characterization in *Beowulf*[49] is the

drawing of parallel portraits so that the juxtaposed descriptions imply through similarity or contrast the essential qualities of a character. Upon first meeting Hygd, the queen of the Geatas, for example, the poet tells us she was not like Thryth and then proceeds to explain who Thryth is and why she is unlike Hygd. The essential contrast between them may be underlined by their quasi-allegorical names. Old English *hygd* means "forethought, reflection," one of the ideal qualities of a Germanic woman, while *þryð* means "force, vehemence," a less queenly quality which proved fatal to the retainers who displeased Queen Thryth.[50]

This appositive method is used repeatedly to characterize Beowulf. After the hero's victory over Grendel, a scop celebrates his prowess by singing not about Beowulf but about two earlier figures from Germanic legend: Sigemund, the prototype of Germanic heroes, and then Heremod, the violent ruler who turned on his own subjects, by whom he was ultimately banished. The point of this curiously indirect way of characterizing Beowulf is never spelled out, but the implication is clear: Beowulf is like Sigemund, unlike Heremod. And here again the names of the two apposed figures signal a contrast. *Sigemund* means "victorious protector" (a precise description of the man who has just saved the Danes from Grendel's depredations), while *Heremod* means "hostile temper" (the defect of character which Beowulf, near the end of his life, prides himself on having avoided [2741–43]).[51] Scholars have seen a similar contrastive intent in the Hama-Hygelac passage in *Beowulf* 1197–1214,[52] and the character Unferth has been seen as existing primarily to serve as a foil to Beowulf.[53]

Characterization is not the only purpose served by significant juxtapositions in *Beowulf*. In 2444–69 the account of an unnamed father grieving for a hanged son is interposed as a parable of Hrethel's grief over Herebeald. A seemingly uncalled-for reflection on how each man must leave the banquet of life and sleep the sleep of death (1002–8) is given relevance by the immediately following description of the actual banquet in Heorot, where all rejoice in blissful ignorance of the death which will soon invade the hall while they are sleeping. In presenting Beowulf's report to Hygelac after the Geatas' triumphant return from Denmark, the poet contrives to have two remarkably similar scenes of royal reception and hospitality stand in proximity, so that as Beowulf recounts the courtly rituals in Heorot (2011–13, 2020–24), those same rituals are being enacted around him in the Geatish meadhall (1976–83). The phrasal echoes between the two passages assure that the audience will sense how the men of old lived in a world of ineluctable recurrence and may even lead some members of the audience to think of fateful parallels between the places and characters juxtaposed: just as Beowulf's valor was needed to save the Danish king's realm, so will it be needed to save Hygelac's realm; just as young Freawaru will lose her husband to old enmities (2065–66), so will young Hygd lose her husband to the strife in Frisia. In another artful juxtaposition the poet places Beowulf's refusal of the Geatish throne (in deference to the young scion of the royal family) alongside the description of the Geatas' war with Onela years later (2373ff.). The resulting contrast displays dramatically the social norm against which Beowulf demonstrates his magnanimity: Onela had banished his nephews and seized the Swedish throne for himself, while Beowulf declines the Geatish throne and acts as protector to his young cousin Heardred, who takes the crown.[54]

I have discussed elsewhere[55] how Beowulf's great speech in 1384–89 acquires much of its power from the poet's simple device of positioning it after the famous description of Grendel's mere. Here it need only be remarked that this narrative collocation is typical of the poet's use of appositive style to express theme. The convictions underlying Beowulf's speech are wholly un-Christian—importance of blood vengeance, personal fame the highest good—but the juxtaposition of the hero's enunciation of his heathen courage with the depiction of the evil forces against which he must prove that courage exacts respect even from an audience which sadly regrets his heathen ignorance of true Christian values. As is the case elsewhere in the poem, the narrator avoids direct comment on the hero's pagan virtue; rather he apposes without comment episodes which force us to admire the men of old no matter how deeply we regret their theological predicament. Here appositive style enables the poet to present pre-Christian heroism honestly yet sympathetically to his Christian world.

Besides narrative segments which stand juxtaposed in *Beowulf*, there are other passages and subjects which seem to stand in a significant but unexpressed relationship even though they are widely separated. The impressive funeral described near the beginning of the poem finds a kind of appositional restatement in the funeral which ends the poem. The symmetry of the two has long impressed scholars as intentional and meaningful, and Klaeber (p. 228) notes that verbal echoes of Scyld's funeral preparations and those for Beowulf further emphasize the implied connection between them. A similar strategy of repeated epithets brings certain characters in the poem into implicit contrast or comparison with each other. Beowulf echoes Unferth's phrasing when he puts forth his version of a story which he wants compared with Unferth's. The aged King Hrothgar and his young champion Beowulf in the first part of the poem seem mirrored by the aged King Beowulf and his young stalwart Wiglaf in the second part, as the formulas which had earlier described the Danish king "æðeling ærgod," "eald eþelweard," "eorla drihten," "folces hyrde," "gumcystum god," "har hilderinc," "frod cyning," "mære þeoden," "rices hyrde," "þeoden mærne") are transferred to old Beowulf, and terms which had been applied to the youthful Beowulf (e.g., "hæle hildedeor," "secg on searwum," and "feþecempa") are inherited by Wiglaf.[56] The poet makes no explicit comment about these significant role shifts, but the symmetry of both character and phrase suggests clearly the inexorable generational cycles in heroic life and the pathos of ageing.

The most forceful expression of the youth-and-age theme in the poem is yet another apposition of narrative segments, the apposition that controls the structure of the entire narrative. *Beowulf* consists of two starkly juxtaposed episodes in the hero's life divided chronologically by a chasm of fifty years and hinged together across that chasm by a single transitional sentence (2200–9). Tolkien describes the structure precisely: "It is essentially a balance, an opposition of ends and beginnings. In its simplest terms it is a contrasted description of two moments in a great life, rising and setting; an elaboration of the ancient and intensely moving contrast between youth and age, first achievement and final death. It is divided in consequence into two opposed portions" (p. 271). From the smallest element of microstructure—the compounds, the grammatical appositions, the metrical line with its apposed hemistichs—to the comprehensive arc of macrostructure, the poem seems built on apposed segments. And the collocation of the segments usually implies a tacit meaning.

If we look beyond the macrostructure of *Beowulf*, we may see one further juxtaposition which is implicit in any reading or rendition of the poem. The highly traditional nature of the subject matter of *Beowulf*, the poet's allusive and sometimes cryptic manner of telling the story, and his frequent abandonment of sequential narration (especially in the last thousand lines) have all persuaded readers from the earliest day of *Beowulf* scholarship that the poem as we have it is a retelling of material familiar to the audience.[57] And an audience perceives a retelling differently from a first telling. On first hearing, people listen for the story; on later hearings they listen for differences between the present and previous versions. Keeping two versions in mind at one time, people notice what the present teller does with the story. Literature as a retelling is of course familiar to students of the Middle Ages, a new treatment of the old story being what most medieval narrative poets purport to be giving to their audiences. But in the case of *Beowulf*, this dimension of the narrative has special significance, since the old stories are ultimately pagan stories and the poet is telling them to a Christian audience which has been warned against too much interest in pagan times. A Christian poet who takes up a narrative such as *Beowulf* would need special tact and sensitivity as a teller, and his audience would probably be alert to his way of handling the old heroes and the old themes.

That the poet was emphasizing that his poem is a retelling is suggested by the fact that he includes so much retelling within *Beowulf*. Repeatedly we are asked to listen to one account of an event and to compare it with another. First Unferth tells the story of Beowulf's swim with Breca, and then Beowulf immediately retells it, asking us to notice the differences, to correct in our minds the inaccuracies of Unferth's telling. Near the end of the first long segment of the narrative dealing with Beowulf's adventures in Denmark, the poet has the hero retell in his own words the events which the poet has just finished narrating himself (1999–2151). Scholars have offered various aesthetic justifications for this curious narrative strategy, but whatever else may have been its purpose, one effect of the retelling is to exercise us once again in comparing narrative versions, in attending to how the poet's own telling differs from the story as it is refracted through the consciousness of Beowulf. The things Beowulf does not include in his version (e.g., the Unferth episode, the sword that failed him, and the defection of the Danes at the mere) give us insights into the hero's magnanimity which are as revealing as the details he adds to the poet's telling (e.g., his identification of the one Geatish casualty as a man named Hondscioh who was dear to him, his sympathetic account of Hrothgar's lamenting his old age at the harp playing, and his concern for the ill-fated marriage between Freawaru and Ingeld). Again the poet forces us to assess a retelling of a known tale when he gives his curiously slanted summary of the scop's story of Finnsburg. We know from the cryptic and omissive way he tells the story that he assumes his audience knows it from another source, and we know from the surviving fragment of *The Fight at Finnsburg* that other tellings of the story were in circulation in Anglo-Saxon England. From a reading of fragment and episode we receive the impression that the original story primarily concerned treachery and revenge for treachery, with the heroic code surviving intact after a severe test. But from the way in which the *Beowulf* poet tells the story, it seems to have more to do with woman's grief in a world of dark-age violence. The theme of vengeance taken and honor preserved is overlaid in the poet's summary with the tragedy of Hildeburh. Since the Finn episode is carefully juxtaposd with Wealhtheow's major scene in the poem—her appeal to Beowulf to support her sons—we can assume that the poet's telling of the story has been shaped for the purpose of stressing a poignant parallel with Wealhtheow's tragic fate, which remains untold in the poem but which was apparently known to the audience. On the level of the factual content of the Finnsburg story as it is represented in the fragment, there is an obvious parallel between the heroic ethos and exploits of the Half-Danes on the one hand and those of the people in Heorot on the other; on the level of the poet's slanted summary, there is an equally obvious parallel between the tragic fates of Hildeburh and Wealhtheow. The Finn lay is appropriate on one level to the public occasion being celebrated in Heorot and on another to the tragic irony which poet and audience see in the future of the Danes. The audience was to entertain simultaneously the emphases of both tellings and to apply each as was appropriate to the situation in Hrothgar's Denmark.[58]

Such exercises in the nuances and emphases of retellings inevitably call our attention to the poet's own strategies of retelling in his management of the narration of *Beowulf*. By planting within his poem significant retellings, he reminds us that, like the scop in Heorot (867ff.), he is putting old sagas (*ealdgesegena*) into new words, and he encourages us to explore the distance between the story he has taken up and his own telling of it. In particular, we have been disciplined by the retold tales within *Beowulf* to heed the poet's perspective on his story as that perspective is conveyed through his own personal use of the poetic language at his disposal. This aspect remains to be examined in my succeeding chapters.

In the present chapter I have tried to suggest that in *Beowulf* the poet is concerned with confronting his Christian nation with the heroic age of their heathen ancestors; that to achieve this confrontation (and ultimately reconciliation) he exploits in a unique way the paratactic, juxtapositional character of Old English poetic style; and that his attention to retellings within his poem repeatedly alerts his audience to the fact that *Beowulf* is itself a retelling and hence his audience must remain sensitive to his own perspective on the characters and events he is presenting. It is noteworthy that these three topics—the appositional style, the theme of present time confronting past time, and the status of *Beowulf* as a retelling of known tales—are all to be found in the majestic opening sentence of the poem:

Hwæt, we Gar-Dena   in geardagum,
Þeodcyninga   þrym gefrunon,
hu ða æþelingas   ellen fremedon!

In form this sentence exemplifies the artfully congested syntax, the heavily nominal surface structure, and the martialing of juxtapositions so characteristic of Old English poetic style. The strong juxtapositional effect of the verse form is highlighted ornamentally, as if the poet were calling his audience's attention to the way verses stand independently in Old English, each hemistich defining itself within its own prosodic boundaries and emphasizing the syntactical appositions which the verses demarcate. The highlighting is achieved through the rhetorical device which Latin rhetoricians term *similiter desinens,* the feature which led ultimately to the development of end rhyme. The chiming suffixes of *þeodcyningas* and *æðelingas* and the repetition of preterite plural endings in *gefrunon* and *fremedon* emphasize the grammetrical pauses and parallelisms of the verse, as if attuning the audience's ear to the binary contrasts and juxtapositions of metrical lines, appositions, and compounds in Old English poetry.

Simultaneously the poet initiates the theme of present time confronting past time. The pronoun *we* unites the audience with the poet in his own time, while the preterite *fremedon,* intensified by the temporal phrase "in geardagum," places the subject of the poem firmly in the past in "days of yore." This emphasis on the contrasting time periods is maintained by various devices throughout the remainder of the poem. The repeated phrase "on þæm dæge þysses lifes" (197, 790, 806) and the phrase "þy dogore" underscore the temporal gulf between Christian present and Germanic past by the abnormal stress on the deictic pronouns.[59] Terms like *fyrndagum,* "in days of old," *fyrnmenn,* "men of old," *ærgeweorc* and *fyrngeweorc,* "works of old," also keep reminding us of the bygone age in which the poem is set, as do, perhaps, the repeated formulas "hyrde ic" and "ic gefrægn" and their variants, which emphasize that we are hearing reports of a distant past.

Finally, the whole point of the opening sentence of *Beowulf* is that the poem is a retelling of exploits already known to the audience. "We have heard[60] of the greatness of the spear-Danes, of kings of nations in days of yore, of how the noblemen wrought deeds of valor." In this characteristically resumptive, appositional sentence reminding us of the great gap of time between the tale and the teller, the poet invites us to read his poem as a pensive reconsideration of things known. The following chapters attempt such a reading.

2. APPOSED WORD MEANINGS
AND RELIGIOUS PERSPECTIVES

In his magisterial edition of *Beowulf,* Frederick Klaeber refers almost despairingly to "the problem of finding a formula which satisfactorily explains the peculiar spiritual atmosphere of the poem" (p. cxxi, n. 2). At times Klaeber thought that the poet sought to "modernize" the pagan society of sixth-century Scandinavia by depicting it as Christian but that his modernization is marred by lapses into historical accuracy, as when the Danes are shown worshiping idols (p. 135). At other times, he thought, perhaps we are to asume that some of the Danes at Heorot were Christians and that they reverted to paganism under the stress of Grendel's attacks.[1] Tolkien insists that the poem is clearly set in pagan Scandinavia and yet sees Hrothgar as a kind of Christian monotheist moving among pagan compatriots.[2] Brodeur too thinks the setting is pagan, but the Christian poet, he feels, would have found it unthinkable that such noble pagans could be damned, and therefore he depicts them as acknowledging the Christian God.[3] Other readers have appealed to allegory or to the naive ahistoricism of the Middle Ages to account for the fact that, although the poem is set in pagan Scandinavia and the poet describes and condemns the pagan rites of the Danes (175–88), the legendary characters often speak with a piety that makes them sound like Christians.[4]

The least persuasive explanations of the problem are those which proceed from an assumption that the poet was vague or absent-minded in his characterization of the religious state of his legendary figures. A Christian Anglo-Saxon, whether in the age of Bede or the age of Ælfric, was not casual or vague-minded about whether a person was Christian or heathen. And the *Beowulf* poet carefully reminds us throughout his poem that the events he is narrating took place in another age and another world. His firm historical sense also rules out Klaeber's suggestion that the poet intends us to think (but neglects to tell us) that there were both Christians and pagans living together in the Northern lands of the heroic age. Both the poet and his audience knew well that sixth-century Scandinavians were heathens.[5] And lest it be thought that Anglo-Saxons tended to forget the heathenism of the Scandinavians as time wore on, we should recall that, in the *Chronicle,* charters, poems, and saints' lives, Old English *hæðen* (as well as Latin *paganus)* was virtually a synonym for *Dene* (i.e., "Scandinavian").[6] Indeed, the association between heathenism and Scandinavians became ever stronger in Anglo-Saxon England as the centuries passed.[7] The vaguely pious heroes of *Beowulf,* then, would not have been mistaken for Christians by an Anglo-Saxon audience.

The obliqueness with which the poet presents his characters' spiritual status, averring that they are pagans and yet presenting them in a way that keeps their paganism in abeyance, is closely consonant with the studied laconism and indirection of the appositive style. It is through this style, I believe, that the poet creates a spiritual setting in which his audience can assess the men of old for what they were. He does not deny his characters' heathenism but uses the traditional diction and appositional effects to free the audience of the mind-numbing alarm which a graphic depiction of a pagan society would cause. He frees them, that is, to reflect, to assess, to sympathize, and even to admire.[8] The mechanism by which he achieves this liberation of judgment is the subject of the present chapter, which will argue that the Cædmonian renovation of Old English poetic diction had left the *Beowulf* poet with a vocabulary in which many words had double meanings—pre-Cædmonian and post-Cædmonian[9]—and that the poet systematically exploited these double meanings to create that "peculiar spiritual atmosphere" remarked by Klaeber. To describe the semantic layering of the Christianized poetic diction of Old English I have indulged in a metaphoric extension of my term "appositive." The term is meant to suggest an analogy between a syntax and narrative structure wherein elements are paratactically (and often ambiguously) juxtaposed and words which carry two "apposed" meanings. In both kinds of apposition, two elements are found together, with no expressed logical connection; just as we must refer to context to construe the syntax and relevance of appositive compounds and unpunctuated clauses, so too we must refer to context to determine how the apposed word meanings are to be understood.

The ambiguous poetic words appear to hold in suspension two apposed word meanings because of the double perspective which the poet maintains throughout *Beowulf*. As the poet's distinctive voice interchanges with the voices of his characters, we strongly sense that we are experiencing the narrative simultaneously from the point of view of the pre-Christian characters and from the point of view of the Christian poet, and either of two senses of ambiguous words seems to be operative, depending on which perspective we adopt. Before examining this ambiguous vocabulary and its bearing on the poem's spiritual atmosphere, it will be necessary to consider the double perspective and how it works in the poem.

In reading *Beowulf* it is important to notice that the monsters are presented from two points of view. To the pagan characters in the poem, these creatures are *eotenas, fifelcynn, scinnan, scynscaþan, scuccan,* and *ylfe*—all terms from pagan Germanic demonology, which the characters (and the poet when he is adopting the characters' perspective) use to refer to the monsters. But the poet in his own voice tells his audience much more about these preternatural creatures, including the true genealogy of the Grendelkin: they are monstrous descendants of Cain, whose progeny was banished by God and punished with the Flood. They are the *gigantas* of the Vulgate, who remain in conflict with the Lord of Heaven. Hrothgar knows nothing of this background (1355–57). Also, the poet, but not the Danes or Geatas, knows that Grendel is God's adversary (786, 1683), a servant of hell (788, 1274), of the Devil's company (756), and feuding with God (711, 811).[10] His term *orcneas,* a hybrid composed of a Latin word for "infernal demon" and a Germanic word for the walking dead,[11] epitomizes the dual perception of the monsters. And this dual perception is of signal importance to our understanding of the poem. When Beowulf, impelled by his heathen ideals of conduct, pits his strength against what he calls a *þyrs* (426), he is unwittingly allying himself with the true God of Christianity in His eternal opposition to diabolic forces of evil. This lends dignity to the heathern hero, who, without knowing it, is fighting on the right side after all.

The poet maintains a dual perception of the monsters by characterizing them in terms which will have meaning in both the Christian and pagan context. The eerie light that "of eagum stod / ligge geli-cost" (726–27) may seem at first to mark Grendel as purely an ogre of Germanic legend, such as the *haugbúi* and other gleaming-eyed monsters of Icelandic saga, but the English life of St. Margaret tells us that when the Devil in dragon's form assaults the saint "of his toþan leome ofstod, . . . and of his eagan swilces fyres lyg."[12] The mere where the Grendelkin dwell seems compact of details from folklore horror tales, and yet we know that it also has unmistakable features drawn from the description of hell in the *Visio Pauli,* which the Blickling Homilist also used. This studied conflation of the demons from Germanic mythology with demons from Christian culture was aided no doubt by the efforts of other Anglo-Saxons to make sense of the parallel demonologies of pagans and Christians. King Alfred in his Boethius translation associates the Titans of pagan Classical mythology with Nimrod and the giants of the Old Testament,[13] while homilists and translators of the Bible sometimes adapted the old Germanic terms for monsters to biblical phenomena.[14] To the characters in the poem *Beowulf,* the monsters have meaning only in terms of the pagan's dark mythology of evil; to the Christian Anglo-Saxons attending the poem this meaning is equally apparent, but they see other meanings as well, because they understand the true nature of evil and its connections with Cain and the Devil.[15] So carefully does the poet maintain this two-leveled portrayal of the monsters that in the last part of the poem he need only introduce a monster with well-established credentials in both worlds—a dra-gon—and trust that the audience will, without further prompting, see the creature in its full complexity. It is on one level of perception like the dragon that Sigemund slew; on another it has those connota-tions of Satanic evil with which Bible and commentary had long invested it.[16]

The same double perspective is maintained, I believe, in the characterization of the heroes in the poem. Their thoughts and their language are circumscribed by the pagan world in which they live, and when at times their speeches seem to have a Christian resonance, the audience is supposed to recognize that these are but coincidences of similar elements in two alien cultures, coincidences which inevit-ably give dignity to the old heroes as viewed by Christian eyes but which betray no Christian revelation in heathen minds. A prime example is the speech which is often tendentiously called "Hrothgar's sermon" (1700–84). Because Hrothgar advises Beowulf against overweening pride, avarice, and irascible violence, some scholars have wanted to see this as a Christian homily on the Seven Deadly Sins, and many parallels in Scripture and commentary have been adduced. But there is nothing in the speech that is not equally accordant with Germanic pre-Christian piety, and there are some things that are appropriate to only such a context. For it is a speech about Germanic leadership, about fame, about the gifts of men, about fulfilling one's destined role in heroic society, about sudden changes of fortune (*edwenden*), and, above all, about how a warrior leader must always purchase the loyalty of his followers with generous gifts. Since people cannot be generous if they are avaricious and cannot monitor their own behavior if they are consumed with arrogance, Hrothgar inevitably warns against vices which Christians also deplore. But this warning bespeaks no Christian illumination mysteriously vouchsafed to a pagan Germanic king. Rather, it reveals a kind of natural, universal wisdom that any noble heathen might share with a Christian. The *Beowulf* poet no doubt emphasized these points where Christian and pagan morality converged in Hrothgar's speech in the hope that the audience would notice them and would marvel that this sixth-century king, though deprived of revelation, could, in his wisdom, strike so close to Christian truths.[17] His doing so would give him dignity and stature in the listeners' estimation, but it would not mislead them into supposing he was a Christian. They would be regretfully aware that he was musing on matters which were ultimately beyond his understanding, since he lacks the theological framework and vocabulary necessary for dealing with them definitively, and, like other pagans, he stands beyond the reach of Christ's redemption. This poignant limitation in Hrothgar's views on moral conduct should be all the clearer to the poem's audience because of the telling description of the king's demeanor as he begins his speech. The poet shows Hrothgar gazing long at the sword hilt with the biblical account of the Deluge engraved upon it. Poet and audience know exactly what the flood that slew the giant race was and whence it came, but Hrothgar does not. Since he has no biblical knowledge, his gaze is a blind gaze. He is in a way like Aeneas gazing at the shield which a god had fashioned for him. The events depicted on the shield are from the future, and Aeneas cannot construe them, but Virgil and his audience could. As with Aeneas, so with Hrothgar, we admire all the more the partial understanding he achieved, since we know that he, unlike us, did not share knowledge with a higher power: "miratur rerumque ignarus imagine gaudent" (VIII, 730).

But this reading of Hrothgar's speech, it may be said, takes no notice of the pious tone of his references to the Deity. Would not his allusions to *Waldend, Metod,* and *mihtig God* mark his disquisition unambiguously as the utterance of a Christian? This question brings us back to the matter of the polysemous vocabulary which resulted from the Christianization of Old English poetic diction by Cædmon and his successors. We may begin with the terms for God which this reformed heroic diction offered the *Beowulf* poet, or at least those terms which he selected for his legendary characters to utter when they referred to a higher being. Usually scholars take the scop's allusion to "se Ælmihtiga" in line 92 as the first time in the poem when a character mentions the Christian God.[18] Actually, it is not the scop who speaks the words "se Ælmihtiga" but the poet who is presenting the song of creation in indirect discourse: "*cwæð þæt se Ælmihtiga eorðan worhte.*" It is reasonable, however, to assume that the poet may have intended us to think that this is the actual term used by the scop for the Creator.[19] But there is no authority whatever for the capital letter *Æ*- which forces modern readers to assume that this allusion refers unambiguously to the Christian Deity. Anglo-Saxon scribes did not capitalize the first letter of *nomina sacra* or of any proper names. Ignoring the modern editors' capitalization in "ælmihtiga," we are free to translate line 92, "He said that the all-powerful one created the earth." Who would the "all-powerful one" be? If the speaker is a heathen, as we should expect the scop in Heorot to be, then "se ælmihtiga" would refer to one of the pagan gods: compare "hinn almáttki áss" in the heathen oath of the Icelanders referring to Thor.[20] Or, if the scop should be not specifically pagan but rather a pre-Christian man of no very specific religious beliefs (somewhat like the nameless atheling who recounts the sparrow simile in Bede's account of the conversion of Edwin), then "se ælmihtiga" might refer to "the all-powerful being (whoever he might be)."[21] Old English *ælmihtig* and its cognates in other Germanic languages obviously did not mean "the Christian God" before contact with Christians, who, upon converting any Germanic nation, usually appropriated the word as a term for God the Father (probably because of its similarity in sense to the Christian Latin *omnipotens*).[22] Such adaptation of pre-Christian vocabulary to Christian concepts was a momentous event in the history of each of the Germanic dialects. Christine Fell has recently pointed out how similar was the development of a Christian terminology for the Deity from pagan diction in Old Icelandic and in Old English: "Snorri, presenting a scholarly critique of poetry, discusses the proper poetic appellations for Christ alongside the proper appellations for heathen gods and earthly kings, and makes it easy for us to see how traditional pre-Christian phrasing and vocabulary could be consciously adapted. When, for example, he points out the ambivalence of a phrase such as 'king of men' or 'king of Jerusalem' which might be used of Christ or a secular king, he is exposing and analysing the process of thought which underlies Cædmon's *moncynnes weard*."[23] In both languages (and presumably in all Germanic languages) the Christianization of the vocabulary was a matter not of the displacement of pre-Christian meanings by Christian meanings but rather of the extension of pre-Christian meanings to include Christian concepts, and so the words retain at least vestiges of early meanings while assuming new Christian senses. Once we remove the capital letter from *ælmihtiga* in *Beowulf* 92, it becomes clear that the word is a polysemous term equally appropriate in pagan and Christian contexts and not, as Hoops and others have assumed, a term specifying the Christian Deity.[24]

Considering the true semantic range of *ælmihtig*, I have said, the heathen scop in Heorot could be referring in line 92 either to a specific Germanic god or to simply "whatever omnipotent one created the earth." The *Beowulf* poet would not be the only Germanic Christian who thought his ancestors may have been capable of sensing the existence of a Creator and of directing their piety toward this dimly perceived Creator rather than toward Germanic gods such as Woden, Thunor, and Tiw. In Icelandic sagas there are several pagan characters who, disregarding the Germanic gods, refer to "the unknown creator" of the world and men, seeming to intuit from their observation of the ordered universe that some supreme being must have been its author.[25] Since the intuitive process of these characters is analogous with the scop's intuition in his hymn to the creator, it may be useful to recall one or two of them here. Arnorr kerlingarnef in the *Flateyjarbók,* for example, suspects that the true God is "he who created the sun to give light and warmth to this earth," and Thorsteinn in *Vatnsdæla saga* speaks of "him who created the sun and the whole world, whoever he may be."[26] Both Arnorr and Thorsteinn are presented as pagan characters moving in a pagan world. The same theme of the exceptionally perceptive pagan who can sense through a kind of instinct or natural goodness the true God behind distortions of paganism can be found among Anglo-Saxon writers. We have already seen that St. Boniface thought that the pagan Saxons and Wends observed the essence of the law and ordinances of God through some mysterious sensing of the truth, and the same is true of the Old English translation of *Orosius.* There, in a considerably elaborated version of the Latin original, the translator says that Caesar Augustus refused to accept credit for the peace that blessed his reign, since only a divine power and not any "eorðlices monnes" deed could have achieved the peace.[27] Earlier in the Old English *Orosius,* Hannibal is described by the translator as understanding, through the agency of a providential rainfall which prevented a battle, that a supreme God was at work.[28] In both of these instances the pagan heroes' sensing of the existence of the true God is an elaboration by the Old English translator of a much vaguer statement by Orosius. Evidently this ennobling view of pre-Christian people of good will was a common one among early Germanic Christians, being shared by the sagamen, St. Boniface, the *Orosius* translator, and, I would suggest, the *Beowulf* poet. The view would have been fostered by Boethius's *Consolation of Philosophy,*[29] and an Anglo-Saxon who knew the *Aeneid* might have fancied that Aeneas's allusion to "the all-seeing mind that knows the right" confirmed the existence of prescient pagans.[30]

Whether the *Beowulf* poet's audience would have taken "se ælmihtiga" as referring to a dim perception of the true God by a pious pagan or as a specific reference to one of the Germanic gods cannot be determined with certainty, and, indeed, the poet may be deliberately leaving the question open, a practice which is characteristic of his appositive strategy. The ensuing passage about the Danes sacrificing to heathen gods (175–83) would incline us toward the assumption that "se ælmihtiga" would mean to the scop the same thing that "hinn almáttki áss" meant to Icelanders in their heathen oath—that is, Thor or one of the other gods. But the fact that the word occurs in a hymn to creation could incline us toward the view that the scop is a noble heathen sensing the presence of a supreme being by observing the ordered workings of the natural world but without any real knowledge of Christianity.[31] The only interpretation of "se ælmihtiga" that would be logically impossible is the one most commonly held by modern students and scholars of the poem, who assume from editors' capitalization of *Ælmihtiga* that this is an unambiguous reference to the Christian Deity and therefore evidence that the scop in Heorot is a Christian. *Beowulf* takes place in a heathen realm in a heathen age, and the scop's creation hymn is one that any pious heathen might sing.[32] The assumption that now and again the heathen characters turn Christian and address themselves to the Christian Deity makes a muddle of the poet's artful strategy of using inherent ambiguities in the Christianized Old English vocabulary to present the men of old favorably and yet honestly to a Christian Anglo-Saxon audience.

The fact that the ambiguity of the vocabulary provides a meaning appropriate to the poem's pagan setting does not mean that the Christian sense of the words is inoperative. "Se ælmihtiga" in line 92 is actually spoken by the *Beowulf* poet, who is reporting the scop's creation hymn in indirect discourse. To the Christian poet the words would necessarily have suggested the specifically Christian meaning as well as the more general pre-Christian sense, which is the only one appropriate for his character, the scop. The poet and his audience lived after that renovation of the Old English poetic language initiated by Cædmon, and for them terms like *ælmihtiga, alwealda, frea, metod,* and *sigora waldend* inevitably suggested the Christian God. But in *Beowulf* the poet is returning that traditional diction of Old English poetry to a pre-Cædmonian, pre-Christian setting where it could have none of the Cædmonian meanings. Therefore, each time the poet's audience heard a character in the poem utter a Christianized Germanic word for a higher being, they would necessarily have had two apposed meanings in mind: the pre-Christian meaning, which was the only one the pagan characters could know, and the postconversion meaning which had become dominant by the time of the poet.[33]

When we imagine the poet's audience sorting through the dual meanings of words and allocating to each the sense appropriate to its context, the process seems at first rather complicated, but in fact it is the same process that goes on throughout the poem as the audience hears nouns describing lord or leader and decides whether an earthly lord or the heavenly lord is meant. *Dryhten* occurs twenty-nine times in *Beowulf*, fifteen times referring to one of the characters in the poem and fourteen times referring to a higher being. But no one would find it complicated to determine whether earthly or heavenly lord is the meaning. When Wiglaf "dryhtne sinne driorigne fand," it can only be his dying king; when the poet says it is well for one "æfter deaðdæge drihten secean," we know he means God. Sometimes Old English poets used the dual meanings of *dryhten* with deliberate punning effect, a notable example being *The Seafarer* 41–43.[34]

It is plausible, then, to assume that the poet's audience had the limberness of mind to differentiate between those contexts which presuppose a pre-Christian meaning for a term for a higher being and those which presuppose a postconversion meaning. When the poet in his own voice refers to "waldendes hyldo" (2292–93), we know he means "the grace of God," for a Christian knows of such Christian doctrines. But *waldend* in other contexts can mean quite different things. In the *Chronicle* poems it refers to English kings,[35] and it can also mean simply "owner" or "master," as in *The Wanderer* 78 and in *Boethius* ("Ælc mon biþ wealdend ðæs ðe he welt").[36] *Waldend* also refers to pagan gods, as when the Old English translator of *Orosius*, in an expansion of his Latin original, describes the deification of Liber: "hi hine æfter hys dæge heom for god hæfdon and hy sædon þæt he wære ealles gewinnes wealdend."[37] We must bear this full range of meanings for *wealdend* in mind when we read Wiglaf's statement that the dead Beowulf must abide in the keeping of *wealdend*: "he longe sceal / on ðæs waldendes wære geþolian" (3108–9). The poet and his audience know that Wiglaf lived before Old English *waldend* had acquired the meaning "Christian God." Would they not then have assumed that for Wiglaf it would have meant something other than what it had come to mean for them? In the sentence just quoted from *Orosius* we also see the word *god* used in a way requiring discrimination of meanings. Since the use of a definite or indefinite article with common nouns is not compulsory in Old English, and since Anglo-Saxon scribes had no convention of capitalizing the first letter of nomina sacra, the words "hi hine . . . for god hæfdon" could be translated either "they had him for a god" or "they had him for God." Context indicates that the former meaning is correct here, since we know that the pagans being spoken of here believed in many gods and did not therefore take Liber Pater for the one supreme God. In other sentences, however, the ambiguity is irresolvable. In the Old English *Orosius*, Book VI, chapter 9, for example, we are told that Domitian "bead þæt mon on gelice to him onbugan scolde swa to gode."[38] Does this mean "he commanded that people should bow down to him as to God" or "he commanded that people should bow down to him as to a god"? Bately capitalizes the *g* of *gode*, indicating that she assumes the first interpretation, but in the earlier edition by Joseph Bosworth[39] the *g* is uncapitalized, and Bosworth translates "they had him for a god" (p. 67). Reference to the Latin original—"dominus sese ac deum uocari scribi colique iusserit"[40]—tells us nothing, for Latin, like Old English, does not require articles before common nouns.[41] Old English terms for the deity like *god*, then, were simply ambiguous. In most cases context removed the ambiguity, but in passages where both pagan and Christian gods are in question, as in the *Orosius* passage just cited or in treatises like the Old English Boethius, where the nature of the god being discussed is itself somewhat problematic, the ambiguities of the word are real and obvious. In the Cotton Otho A.vi manuscript of *The Consolation of Philosophy*, for example, we find the Old English scribe himself puzzling over whether *god* represents the name of the Christian Deity or the common noun *gōd* "the good." He often tries to make a distinction by marking the vowel of *gōd* long or by doubling the vowel, but as Sedgefield notes in the glossary of his edition, "the two are occasionally confused, *God* being written *good* or *gód*."[42]

The ambiguity of words like *ælmihtig, alwalda, dryhten, god*, and *metod*, which have a pre-Cædmonian meaning coexisting with a postconversion Christian meaning, was, I believe, seized upon by the *Beowulf* poet and was artfully exploited in a way that is characteristic of his style of appositional reticence in telling the tale of Beowulf.

By restricting his names for the higher being(s) to words which have
two possible referents, Christian and pre-Christian, and then placing
these words in a poem in which simultaneous Christian and
pre-Christian contexts are pervasively present, he has solved in a way
that is seriously meaningful the problem that is central to his theme
of cultural reconciliation, the problem of what to call the supernatural forces to which the characters in the poem appeal. To give them
Christian names like *Christ, Hælend, Nergend,* or *Halig Gæst* would
be patently absurd. To revive the Germanic pantheon and speak of
Woden, Tiw, and *Thunor* would shock a Christian audience and
would invite censorship from Christian copyists. More seriously, it
would alienate the poet's audience from the very world to which it is
his purpose to reconcile them. He solves the dilemma by exploiting
the ambiguities of a poetic diction which had been semantically
stratified by the Cædmonian renovation. A further example will help
clarify some of the details of his strategy.

When Beowulf and his Geatisc companions complete their
voyage to Denmark, we are told, "Gode þancedon / þæs þe him
yþlade eaðe wurdon" (227–28). And the modern editors' invariable
practice of capitalizing the first letter of *Gode* creates the problem so
often remarked by critics: how could pagan Geatas pray to the
Christian God? But when we return to the original, uncapitalized
form of the manuscript, we can translate the sentence, "They gave
thanks to a god for the fact that the ocean journey had been an easy
one." That is the meaning of the sentence in the context of the pagan
world inhabited by the characters in the poem. But another context is
simultaneously present: the shared world of poet and audience,
which is the Christian world. Speaking, as it were, over the heads of
his pagan characters, the poet often addresses specifically Christian
comments to his Christian contemporaries, remarking sadly that the
spiritual ignorance of the men of old will cost them an eternity in hell
(183–88), explaining the biblical origins of Grendel (104–14, 1258–
67), alluding to the Old Testament account of the Deluge with a
cryptic brevity which bespeaks confidence of shared information
(114, 1689–91), and reiterating regularly that God ruled the world
in the days of the men of old (who were ignorant of Him) just as He
rules it now. In this Christian context embracing poet and audience,
any occurrence of *god* (or of *metod, alwalda,* or *frea,* etc.) will

inevitably suggest the Christian meaning. So, when the poet says that Beowulf and his men "gode þancedon," the Christian audience knows that on the level of the characters in the poem, with their limited perception and their pre-Cædmonian diction, the noun could only refer to whatever god they knew—Thunor or Woden or perhaps "him who created the sun and the whole world, whoever he may be." But on the level of the poet and his audience, it is commonly known who the supreme being really was at the time when the Geatas were addressing their thanks to whatever god they perceived. Perhaps poet and audience felt about the heathen gods as St. Boniface and his fellow missionaries are said to have felt when they confronted, with sorrow and compassion, the heathen Saxons worshiping their deities: "The heathen gods were, after all, dim adumbrations of the one Divine Being, 'ignorantly worshipped.' "[43] The pervasive homonymy in Anglo-Saxon words for a higher being was ideally suited to a poet who wished to affirm the distance between Christian contemporaries and noble pagan ancestors while simultaneously poeticizing a kind of cultural-linguistic fellowship between the two. It is this homonymy which enables the poet to achieve his complex and moving tone of mingled admiration and regret.

Despite the stern anathemas of an Alcuin or an Augustine, there were men of comprehensive sympathies who, though not blinking at the inevitable destiny of pagans, did strain to envision them with compassion. We see this in Minucius Felix's observation that "those who would see Jupiter as the all-ruler are mistaken in the name, yet they agree there is a single highest power," and we see it in the Second Vatican Mythographer's suggestion that a single god is the reality underlying Sol, Apollo, Diana, and the other divine names of the pagans; and, most important, we can, according to one recent study, see it on Germanic soil in Snorri's prologue to the *prose Edda*.[44] Evidently the early Christian view that pagan gods were simply disguises of the devil coexisted with conceptions of the pagan gods as imperfect realizations of the true Deity or as mistaken names for what would later be identified as God. Amid such various conceptions of the nature of pagan gods, it is not surprising that the *Beowulf* poet should discern in the historically based ambiguities of Old English poetic diction a strategy for representing in a complex and sympathetic way the pagans' theological gropings.

At a later stage in the Middle Ages, Dante faced an analogous problem in his portrayal of the good pagan Virgil. Introducing himself as one who lived "in the time of the false and lying gods" ("nel tempo de li dei falsi e bugiardi," *Inferno* I, 72), Virgil refers to the Christian God in the only terminology he knows. Christ harrowing hell is simply "a mighty one" ("un possente," *Inferno* IV, 53), and God the Father is "that Emperor who reigns above" ("quello Imperador che lassu regna," *Inferno* I, 124). Dante and his audience could admire the great poet as he makes his respectful, vague references to God, while at the same time they would feel the poignancy of his limited vision of that God. (Another device used by both Dante and the Beowulf poet is the unwitting scriptural allusion: Hrothgar [942–46] and Virgil [*Inferno* VIII, 45] both echo Luke 11:27 but in pathethic ignorance that they are doing so.) With Dante, as with the *Beowulf* poet, the aim is for noble pagans to use terms for the higher being which are historically appropriate to the speaker but at the same time close enough to the Christian religious vocabulary to soften the focus on pagan piety. A partial analogy in the modern world would be a novel written by an English-speaking Christian about pious Moslems. If the novelist's purpose were to distance his Moslem characters from his Christian audience and to emphasize their exotic infidelism, he might portray them calling on Allah or Mohammed, ritually facing Mecca, and practicing polygamy. If his purpose on the other hand were to induce his readers to sympathize with the Moslems in the narrative, he might avoid detailing the more exotic rites of Islam and translate *Allah* into "God." Such a translation would not misrepresent the religious condition of the Moslems, for the audience would know that their religion is not that of the Christians, and they would know that the Arabic word for God and the Moslem conception of God differ from the Christian. But the polysemy of the word *god* would accommodate both the Christian and the Moslem conceptions without confusing the two. In *Beowulf* a poet is working in a somewhat similar way to accommodate the pagan forebears to the Christian world view of the Anglo-Saxons.

The *Beowulf* poet's pervasive play on the dual meanings of names for a higher being in the poem is possible, of course, only because he has selected with such meticulous care the terms that his characters use in their references to the deity they address. Specifically Christian terms for Christ, the Holy Ghost, and the Trinity (which are ubiquitous in the poetry of Cynewulf, the anonymous religious poets, and the various Christian narratives) are scrupulously avoided by the *Beowulf* poet. The popular system of God terms consisting of a base word combined with the genitive *engla* ("*engla cyning,*" "*helm engla,*" "*heofonengla cyning,*" and so forth) are never used by the characters in *Beowulf,* who refer instead to "*ylda waldend*" (1661), "*sigora waldend*" (2875).[45] An even more popular expression for the Christian Deity is the system of two-part terms meaning "God's Son," such as "*godes bearn,*" "*godes gastsunu,*" and "*sunu dryhtnes.*" Referring too specifically to the second person of the Trinity, these are also avoided completely by the *Beowulf* poet.[46] The terms *nergend* and *hælend,* which occur more than 150 times in poetry outside *Beowulf* (including even some Old Testament poetry) are never used by characters in *Beowulf,* apparently because they are too specifically associated with the Savior Christ. *Milde,* which Keiser notes is an especially frequent epithet of the Christian Deity,[47] is never used of a deity in *Beowulf.* Just as he never alludes to the Incarnation, Crucifixion, Eucharist, Redemption, Cross, church, saints, New Testament, and other cardinal elements of Christianity, the poet avoids with remarkable consistency any God terms which are specifically or exclusively Christian in their denotation, preferring instead the more equivocal terms such as *alwalda, fæder alwealda, frea ealles,* and *metod.*

Having created this artfully ambiguous terminology for his pagan characters to use, the poet himself often echoes their vague terminology in his own references to God, thus reducing the verbal impact of his theological alienation from the men of old. His purpose being to reconcile Christian Anglo-Saxons poetically to their pious but pagan forebears, he adopts the God terms of his pre-Christian characters when he refers to God himself, giving an illusion of superficial respectability to his characters, but an illusion which is poignantly transparent.[48]

But the poet's terminology for the deity is not wholly undifferentiated from that of his heathen characters. The Christian God whom the poet and audience worship is not the same as the gods of the Germanic pantheon or as the heathens' vague premonitions of God, and the poet must make this clear. He does so repeatedly, but, except for the anguished contrasting of pagan with Christian deity in 175–88, his distinctions between the two are made in a subdued tone which does not disrupt the superficial harmony between the piety of his own day and that of the men of old. Typically the distinction is drawn in passages where heathen (or diabolic) power is operative, and the poet is concerned to emphasize that although the forces of evil enjoyed supernatural powers (as medieval Christianity readily acknowledged), this must not confuse us as to who the real God is.

When the blood of Grendel melts the blade of the giant sword in 1605–8, the poet says that it was a notable marvel or miracle ("þæt wæs wundra sum," 1607).[49] But he then hastens to contrast this miracle of the diabolic forces with the much greater miracle of the true God, who controls the times and seasons of the world: "Þæt is soð metod" (1611). Similarly, when he describes the preternaturally powerful curse laid on the gold of the dragon's hoard by a heathen charm (3051–52), he adds that its power can be overturned at any time by the greater power of "god sylfe, sigora soðcyning" (3054–55). Only the poet in his own voice uses the modifiers *soð* and *self* with terms for God, for these are the words which Old English writers habitually use to differentiate the true God of Christianity from the false gods of the heathen. Thus in Cynewulf's *Juliana* the pagan gods *(hlafordas, halgum, godu,* etc.) are contrasted with *soðne god, soðcyning.* And in *Azarias* 44–48, Azarias asks God to reveal his power so that the heathen may know "þæt þu ana eart . . . soð meotod," and elsewhere in the poetry *soð* is one of the commonest epithets of the Christian God as distinguished from spurious heathen deities.[50] In prose the word *soð* is also frequently used to contrast the Christian God with pagan gods. In Ælfric's and Wufstan's interdependent homilies *De falsis diis*, pagan deities are differentiated from the God of Christendom, who is described as "se an soða god."[51] In the Old English *Orosius, soð* is regularly used to differentiate the God of the Christians from heathen deities, as when the Egyptians are said to attribute certain miracles to "hiora agnum godum" and "nales þam soþan gode,"[52] or when the Romans seek through sacrifices to recruit the help of their gods, who, says Orosius, "næs na se soða god."[53] Even more familiar will be Bede's story of the conversion of Edwin, in which "þam soðan gode" and "þæs soðan godes" occur repeatedly to distinguish the Christian God of

Paulinus from the pagan gods whom Cefi had worshiped.[54] Here the term is a translation into Old English of Bede's *verus deus*, which in Christian Latin often serves to specify the Christian God. Gregory the Great uses it so in his letter to Abbot Mellitus, where the Pope contrasts the worship of God with the pagan Anglo-Saxons' worship of the devil.[55]

The other epithet which the poet uses of God but which his characters never use is *self*. This too is a traditional way of distinguishing the God of Christendom from heathen gods, both in poetry[56] and in prose, as in the twelfth *Vercelli Homily*, which says that when the pagans approached the idols which devils had occupied, "Þonne tealdon men þæt þæt wære god sylfa; wæron þæt þonne þa wyrrestan hellegæstas, nalas god sylfa, ælmihtig eallra gesceafta Scippend."[57] Similarly, Ælfric has St. Crysanthus contrast the powers of his Christian God with those of pagan idols: "Me fylste god sylf mid godcundre mihte. Þine godas ne geseoþ ne soðlice ne gehyrað ac syndon andgitlease mid leade gefæstnode."[58] Both *soð* and *sylf* are used in the Exeter Book *Maxims* where the poet is distinguishing between the pagan and Christian gods: "Woden worhte weos," he says, contrasting Woden with the ruler of the spacious heavens ("rume roderas"). Then he adds, "þæt is rice god, / sylf soðcyning, sawla nergend, / . . . þæt is meotud sylfa" (133–37). The use of terms like "god sylf," *soðcyning*, and "meotud sylfa" was, then, a common way of distinguishing God from false gods, and the *Beowulf* poet's use of them for this purpose reminds us of the ambiguous status of the terms for a higher being used by the heroes of the poem.

The reference in the Exeter *Maxims* to God as wielder of "rume roderas" introduces another means by which Anglo-Saxons specify the true God as opposed to pagan deities. In *Beowulf* only the poet refers to a God of the Heavens ("heofena helm" in 182, "rodera rædend" in 1555); his characters do not know the dwelling place of the true God, "for all the gods of the nations are idols, but the Lord made the heavens" (Psalm 96:5). Ignorance of where the true God dwells is a characteristic of the virtuous heathen that is noted by Snorri in his preface to the *Prose Edda:* "They knew not yet where his kingdom was; but this they believed: that he ruled all things on earth and in the sky."[59] In Old English poems about Christians or Jews striving against heathens, "God of the heavens" is often used to specify the true God,[60] and in later saints' lives the God who is "in heaven" is frequently so distinguished (possibly with an echo from the Lord's Prayer) from the false gods of the heathen.[61] The *heofonlice* God is contrasted with the gods of the heathen in *De falsis diis* as well.[62]

There are, then, distinctions between the theological language of the poet and that of his pagan characters, but the distinctions are deliberately muted by the preponderance of terms which are shared by the poet with his characters but which carry different meanings, depending on which of the two contexts applies. This is the poet's characteristic method for dealing with the theological tensions in the poem, and it bears further exemplification and analysis. In the two sentences foretelling the outcome of the fight with Grendel, the poet says,

> Ac him dryhten forgeaf
> wigspeda gewiofu, Wedera leodum,
> frofor ond fultum, þæt hie feond heora
> ðurh anes cræft ealle ofercomon,
> selfes mihtum. Soð is gecyþed,
> þæt mihtig god manna cynnes
> weold wideferhð.   [696–702]

Commentators have been eager to dismiss the overt pagan allusion "wigspeda gewiofu,"[63] but it would seem to function here precisely according to the poet's usual strategy with theological language. From the perspective of Beowulf and his men, the victory they achieve will seem to be a woven web of destiny granted to them by a *dryhten*.[64] But the poet knows that *dryhten* with a different meaning is the true source of their success, and that it is His help and support ("frofor and fultum") that give victory to the Geatas, although they cannot know it. The phrases "ðurh anes cræft" and "selfes mihtum" refer not, I suspect, to Beowulf, as is usually assumed, but to *dryhten*, "anes . . . selfes" carrying here that specialized meaning of "the one true God" discussed above. The poet implies here the familiar Augustinian notion that the true God has always ruled men's ways, helped and guided them, even when they did not know of Him:

> Soð is gecyþed,
> þæt mihtig god manna cynnes
> weold wideferhð.   [700–2]

This important idea, which is expressed repeatedly at crucial points in *Beowulf,* is also seen in the Old English *Orosius,* where again and again it is urged that God's hand can be discerned in history, directing the affairs of men even when they were unaware of Him and sacrificing to idols. There is also something of the Boethian view here: what men in pre-Christian times took as the weavings of fate or wyrd was actually God's providence. Here again the poet contrives to gain dignity for his characters, suggesting that they were interacting with God and even enjoying His support, although they could not know it and were, of course, beyond His salvation.

We see the same double perspective in the sentence describing the thoughts of the Geatas as they await Grendel's attacks:

> Þæt wæs yldum cuþ,
> þæt hie ne moste, þa metod nolde,
> se s[c]ynscaþa under sceadu bregdan   [705–7]

At the pre-Christian characters' level of perception, this is the Germanic warrior's familiar commonplace of grim consolation in mortal danger: like Sǫrli in *Hamðismál,* they knew that "no man outlives the evening after the Norns' decree,"[65] or, to state the sentiment positively, the men knew that they could not be killed if Fate had not ordained it. But the old heathen sense of *metod* (Fate, the Measurer) had been overlaid in Christian times by the meaning "Lord" (the Christian God), and poet and audience know that it is *metod* in this sense that was truly presiding over the conflict in the poem, determining whether the warriors should survive or die.[66] In the past scholars have attended to only one level or the other of the sentence's meaning rather than to both, and as a result conflicting interpretations have resulted. A. J. Wyatt, for example, prints *metod* with a lower-case *m,* implying that he sees only the characters' understanding of the sentence, while Klaeber and others capitalize the first letter of *Metod,* signaling a Christian version of the statement. The Geatas' pre-Christian sense of the passage is a primitive, inchoate version of the full sense perceived by poet and audience in light of their fuller understanding gained through revelation. Both levels of perception are operative in the poem, but each must be appreciated in its proper context.

We see *metod* operating in this homonymous way in direct discourse as well as in reported speech. In his monologue before engaging the dragon, Beowulf says that the outcome of the battle shall be "swa unc wyrd geteoð, / metod manna gehwæs" (2526–27): "as wyrd, the measurer of each person, shall decree for us." This surely is the meaning that the words have for Beowulf, and editors like von Schaubert who specify that *metod* here means "fate" are clearly right.[67] And yet Klaeber and others who insist that *metod* means "(Christian) God" are also right; they are simply viewing Beowulf's statement from the perspective of the narrating poet, for whom "metod manna gehwæs" could only seem like an appositive gloss to "wyrd," explaining providentially the true nature of wyrd, which, as Christians knew, was but the accomplishment of God's determinations. "Metod eallum weold / gumena cynnes, swa he nu git deð," says the poet (1057–58), but *metod* has undergone a momentous semantic change since the time when He was presiding over the noble heathens of the tale of Beowulf, and this, I believe, poet and audience fully understood.[68]

Aldhelm understands it when, in his seventh enigma, 3–4, he has a personified Fate say, "The Ancients falsely named me mistress, who swayed the scepter of the world until the Grace of God assumed command."[69] In his verse tract on virginity, moreover, Aldhelm often uses pagan Classical epithets for the Deity, expecting his readers to recognize the Virgilian or Horatian origins of his verbal finery while simultaneously supplying the proper Christian referent, which the context of his treatise requires. This use of pre-Christian terminology for higher beings is perhaps more commonplace among Anglo-Saxons than we usually realize. Even in the Anglo-Saxon charters we find opening formulas like "in nomine altitonantis mundi satoris," "in nomine summi tonantis," and "ego Eadwig largiflua summi tonantis providentia rex Anglorum."[70] And Christian-Latin poets like Arator and Prudentius, who were popular in Anglo-Saxon England, made similar use of terms like *tonans* and *numen* to refer to the Christian God even while using the same terms in the same works to refer to pagan gods.[71] In one English manuscript of Arator and Prudentius, moreover, we actually encounter an Anglo-Saxon reader analyzing these classical terms for deities to distinguish places where the words refer to pagan gods from those where they refer to the Christian God: over forms of *tonans*, "thunderer," and *numen*, "divinity," he writes *deus, creator, verbum dei*, or "christus vel deus" when the terms refer to the Christian Deity, while superscribing *idola, fictiles dei,* or "dei vel simulacra" when the same terms refer to the false gods.[72] These glosses show an Anglo-Saxon reading a poetic text in just the way that I am suggesting *Beowulf* would have been read. Had the Cambridge glossator turned his attention to *Beowulf,* he might well have found himself pondering the same ambiguities that resulted when Arator and Prudentius use originally pagan terms for the Christian God, but in this case it would be pagan Germanic terms. But in applying his differentiating glosses to *Beowulf,* he would have to have decided whether he was viewing each god name from the perspective of the character who spoke it or from that of the poet who was putting the word in the character's mouth.

Reading *Beowulf* is, in a way, like reading the centos of Proba, Luxorius and Pomponius, who composed entire poems on Christian subjects by rearranging the verses of Virgil, Horace, and Ovid in order to make them convey Christian meanings. Students of these curious works hold two contexts in mind at the same time, for their pleasure is in following the Christian level of the narrative while remaining aware of the source of the poetic language. Just as in reading the centos we think simultaneously of Aeneas and Christ, so in reading *Beowulf* we should hear distant echoes of Thunor and Woden when the men of old appeal to their "mihtig dryhten" and "fæder alwalda." We know to whom these words refer in the Christian present, but we also know that they once referred to other, darker beings.[73]

The theological vocabulary of *Beowulf* undergoes a centolike transformation in reverse when the poet locates his story with its Christianized Germanic diction back in a pre-Christian, pre-Cædmonian era. It is quite simply the dramatic setting of the poem that reactivates the non-Christian meanings of words. And lest the audience be unmindful of these meanings, the poet at times builds into his text reminders of pre-Christian meanings by using words in contexts which delimit their semantic range to exclusively pre-Christian reference. In the compound *metodsceaft,* used once by Wealhtheow and once by the dying Beowulf, *metod* can only mean "fate," and the simplex *metod* in 2527 is forced to have a predominantly pagan meaning because it is placed in apposition to *wyrd.*[74] These usages of the word, occurring alongside usages in which the sense is clearly and exclusively the Christianized one (e.g., 110, 1057), en-sure that when readers encounter the word in statements like Beowulf's comment "Ic hine ne mihte, þa metod nolde, / ganges getwæman," they will have both meanings in mind and will under-stand that one meaning fits the world of the dramatic speaker, while another is suggested to the Christian audience. Should they fail to respond to the play of double sense in this passage, the poet adds a further jog to memory, stating in 1611, "þæt is soð metod." This reminds us overtly that there is a true Christian metod as well as a false pre-Christian metod in question and that we must keep both in mind.

Again, when Hrothgar says in 945 that *ealdmetod* was favorable to Beowulf's mother when she bore him, he is thinking no doubt of "the ancient measurer, the ancient dispenser," or simply "fate." To a Christian hearing the word, however, it would carry the further meaning "God of old." In the peculiar context of *Beowulf*, moreover, the word may well have suggested a third and troubling import: Hrothgar has indeed invoked the "old" metod in contrast to the new metod. Such interplay of significations comes easily in *Beowulf* not only because the poet restricts his God terminology so carefully but also because of the appositive style. The ubiquitous variations play-ing off one term against the other, activating one meaning of a word in one passage and another in a different passage, tease us into a constant alertness to the semantic layering of words, much as Shakespeare's puns and quibbles attune his audience's ears to the more serious resonances of Elizabethan English. (In chapter 3 I shall deal in more detail with the mechanics and effects of apposition.)

As D.H. Green reminds us, several scholars have noted the analogy between the Christianization of the Old English vocabulary and the early missionaries' conversion of pagan shrines to Christian uses, following the advice that Pope Gregory gave to Abbot Mellitus.[75] The analogy is sound, for in both renovations the result is a fusion of Christian with pre-Christian elements: Anglo-Saxon Christianity supersedes the old lore but is content to subsist with echoes from the past. The accommodation of the two could go awry, as when King Rædwald erected within the same temple one altar to Christ and another to the old pagan gods. If disproportions occur in the Christian-pagan accommodation in the poetic language, it is probably in the opposite direction of underemphasizing the pagan element, at least in the diction of *Beowulf*. For at times the poet, in his efforts to lend dignity to the heroes' piety, seems to err on the side of Christianizing their piety. Once Beowulf refers to "ecum dryhtne" (2796), and a modern reader might object that the gods of the Northmen, so far as we can tell from Icelandic sources, were mortal, not *ece* (i.e., "eternal"). But such an objection would probably impart to the adjective *ece* a specificity which is unwarranted. In Ælfric's first letter to Wulfstan, *ece* describes the material to be used for making a chalice and apparently means simply "lasting, durable."[76] In *Exodus* 370 "ece lafe" is the "lasting remnant" on Noah's ark, the specimens of the various creatures from which postdiluvian generations will spring. In the Old English *Orosius*, *ece* modifies *þeowas* where we are told that the Samnites wanted to make the Romans their perpetual slaves or their slaves for life.[77] In *Paris Psalter* 64:9, "eceum wæstmum" appears to mean "lasting fruits," while "ece gear" in 76:5 means "years of old" ("of yore, of old" being one of the senses of the *Vulgate aeternus*). In *Beowulf*, *ece* modifies *eorðreced*, the dragon's lair. Beowulf's "ecum dryhtne" in 2796, then, may have meant nothing more to the dying hero than "the enduring prince" or "the prince of old." It is only with Cædmonization of the vocabulary that "ece dryhten" assumes the unvarying sense of "eternal Lord."

Tolkien was troubled by the phrase "godes leoht geceas" (2469), spoken by Beowulf as he recounts the death of Hrethel. Are these words wholly inappropriate in the mouth of a pre-Christian Geat? In both Old English and Old Icelandic *leoht* (OIcel. *ljós*) can have the metaphorical sense of "a region or condition." An expression for "to die" is "fara í ljós annat", "go to the other region or condition." Beowulf's comment "gumdream ofgeaf, godes leoht geceas" could be simply a variation of the standard periphrasis, carrying the meaning "he left the joys of men and sought out the realm of a god." We might even take the expression literally, if Icelandic mythology is to be trusted as a representation of general Germanic beliefs about the next world. *Vǫluspá* 64:2 tells us that the hall Gimlé, which is "sólu fegra" ("brighter than the sun"), is where good men shall go after death, and Snorri reiterates the point in the *Prose Edda*.[78] Other halls of the gods are also described as brilliant with light, *Breidablik*, meaning "broad-gleaming," and *Glitnir,* meaning "glittering." And the light elves are prominent in the realm of the Norse gods. Since the poet's strategy seems to be to dwell on those aspects of pre-Christian beliefs which are least in conflict with Christian culture, it is possible that he chose "godes leoht geceas" as a phrase which could be justified in terms of Germanic pagan mythology while at the same time having, by happy chance, a certain Christian resonance.

A more complex case is that of Old English *dom.* This is at once a most Christian and a most pagan word.[79] When the poet says in his own voice, "Swa hit oð domes dæg diope benemdon / þeodnas mære" (3069–70), we may be fairly sure that in the poet's mind "domes dæg" refers to the purely Christian concept of the Last Judgment. But elsewhere the word *dom* is used eleven times with the earlier meaning "fame"—the (good) judgment which is passed on men's deeds by posterity and which affords a man the only life beyond death he can be sure of in a pagan world. Beowulf articulates this view most clearly when he says,

> wyrce se þe mote
> domes ær deaþe;   þæt bið drihtguman
> unlifigendum   æfter selest.   [1387–89]

Three times it is used in another traditional Germanic sense: Beowulf, Sigemund, and Wiglaf on different occasions each receive a reward of treasure according to "selfes dom" ("their own judgment")—that is, the maximum amount. In all these occurrences the meaning of *dom* poses no difficulty. Twice, however, Beowulf uses the word in contexts which have been taken by some readers to be references to the Last Judgment—a problematic reading, since the pre-Christian hero could have had no knowledge of Christian eschatology. In 977–79, Beowulf says that when the wounded Grendel returns to the mere, there in his cave he must await "miclan domes, hu him scir metod scrifan wille." Earlier Beowulf had said that when he and Grendel fought, the loser, who dies, will have to accept "dryhtnes dome" (441). Contrary to prevailing opinion, I do not believe that these are references to the Last Judgment. Rather Beowulf is saying that combatants who suffer defeat have to resign themselves to the decision of the god who determines when people shall die. A similar idea is expressed by Beowulf in 685–86, where he says that if Grendel joins battle with him, then

> witig god
> on swa hwæþere hond   halig dryhten
> mærðo deme,   swa him gemet þince.   [685–87]

That is, the wise god, the divine lord, will assign the glory of victory
on whichever side seems to him proper. In Old Icelandic literature
dómr often refers to the decision of a higher (pagan) power as to
when a person shall die. We see this sense in the compound *Norna-
dómr*, the decision of the three Norns who control both the fate of
the world and the individual fate of each man. *Skapa-dómr*, "the
judgment of fate," has a similar sense. In poetry this usage yielded a
formula for "to die"—*njóta Norna dóms*" ("to undergo the judgment of the Norns"). When Beowulf says, then, that Grendel, after
his defeat, "must await the great decision as to what the manifest
ordainer will decree for him," he would appear to be using a Germanic formula for dying. (It would seem pointless to say he must wait to
see how he fares in the Last Judgment, since the poet has been specific
and repetitive in asserting Grendel's sure damnation.) Similarly,
when Beowulf says before the combat that the loser will have to
resign himself to the doom of the lord, he is saying what any Germanic warrior might appropriately say.[80] The poet's Christian audience might well be reminded of Christian Doomsday by these death
formulas of Beowulf's, but they would not assume that Beowulf
would be aware of this overtone. Rather they would probably feel
pity for a noble heathen who faces death without true understanding
of what that death means.

The discussion thus far has centered largely on the polysemous
nature of the *Beowulf* poet's terms for God and God's determinations, but the same semantic layering of Christian and pre-Christian
senses is present in much of the poetic language at large. Sometimes
the context activates one sense, sometimes another, but in all cases
the apposed meanings are present *in posse*, and each time the audience privileges one meaning of a word and suppresses another, it is
reminded of the theological contrast between itself and the characters in the poem, for that contrast has been incorporated into the
poetic language itself. The word *mægen*, for example, had both
Christian and non-Christian meanings in Old English. Modern editors in their glossaries tell us that the only meaning the word has in
Beowulf is "strength, might," since these are the qualities the hero

needs in his struggles with men and monsters.[81] But I wonder whether the minds of Anglo-Saxons listening to *Beowulf* were as linguistically compartmentalized as an editor's glossary. To a Christian Anglo-Saxon, *mægen* was a single word with a single continuum of meanings. The basic sense was "physical strength," but there are derived senses relating to various kinds of power, including the Christian sense "virtue" (a development parallel to that in the Latin *virtus* as it was used by Christian Latin writers).[82] Since the Christian sense "virtue" had become a part of the word's meaning, presumably the audience of *Beowulf* could not but feel the presence of that sense even when it encountered *mægen* referring to physical strength. And each time the listeners' minds registered the irrelevance of the Christian sense, there was a momentary, flickering recognition of the fact that the noble race whose deeds they were admiring was, after all, distanced from the audience by a gulf of tragic ignorance.

An important, recurrent expression of the *Beowulfian* narrative perspective is the statement that the hero "wæs moncynnes mægenes strengest / on þæm dæge þysses lifes" (196–97; cf. 789–90, 806). "He was of all mankind the strongest in strength *(mægen)* in *that* day of *this* life." As Roberta Frank has now observed, the temporal distance between pagan past and Christian present is skillfully emphasized by the abnormal alliterative stress on *þam* and *þysses*.[83] Less skillful, we might think, is the apparent tautology "strongest in strength." But consideration of the apposed meanings "strength" and "virtue" which inhere in *mægen* may lead us to a fuller appreciation of this half-line. Remembering that the word which could mean "Christian virtue" to the audience meant only "physical strength" in Beowulf's day, we may suspect that, to a contemporary of the poet's, the sentence could have meant something like "He was of all mankind the strongest in what passed for virtue in that day of this life."[84] Only for the characters in the poem would there have been a tautology; for poet and audience the increment of meaning which the word *mægen* had attained by their day would have made "mægenes strengest" significantly contrastive, especially with the following line "on þæm dæge þysses lifes," emphasizing the two distinct periods of Anglo-Saxon history.

The numerous subsequent occurrences of *mægen* would have had something of the same dual significance. When Hrothgar, proclaiming Beowulf's fitness for kingship, says to the young hero, "þu eart mægenes strang ond on mode frod," the audience, perceiving the nontautological sense of the phrase, recognizes that Beowulf *is* virtuous as well as strong in Hrothgar's sense, but he is lacking in awareness of his virtue's source and nature. Again, Wiglaf says of Beowulf's desperate predicament on his death-day, "Nu is se dæg cumen / þæt ure mandryhten mægenes behofað" (2646–47). To the poem's audience, Wiglaf says more than he realizes: Beowulf's death day is indeed the day when he has need of Christian virtue. But since he exercises his prowess on the far side of the semantic change which gave Christian meaning to *mægen*, Beowulf's greatest need cannot possibly be met.

In an earlier passage *mægen* interacts with another word which has both Christian and pre-Christian meanings. Explaining how Beowulf prevailed in the fight with Grendel, the poet says, "He gemunde mægenes strenge,/ gimfæste gife, ðe him god sealde" (1270–71). In pre-Christian times *gife* meant "gift," pure and simple, but with Christianization of the vocabulary it came to serve simultaneously as the common term for Christian grace.[85] While Beowulf, with his pre-Christian meanings, thinks that the only gift that a god has given him is his physical strength, the Christian audience knows that the real gift that God offers is grace, and that grace, if understood, enables a person to recognize and practice the virtue requisite for salvation. The poet repeats this interplay of meanings in lines 670 and 2182, exploiting there the double sense of *hyldo* and *metod* as well as of *mægen*.

Words like *mægen*, in which dual semantic layers are activated by the dual perspectives in the poem, illustrate that the play of double sense in *Beowulf* is not simply a matter of recalling pre-Christian senses of words but also of bringing to a reader's experience of the poem the Christian meanings which developed after the period of the poem's present time. If we read *Beowulf* bearing in mind its diction's full range of meaning, compounds and phrases like *mægencræft* and *mægenes cræft*, *mægenstrengo* and *mægenes strenge*, all of which have been designated "tautological" compounds or phrases, are invested with contrastive meaning and a slight situational irony by the dual perspectives in the poem.[86]

The early need for an Anglo-Saxon vocabulary of iniquity in the

Christian context also led to words of dual meaning. Two high-frequency words meaning "sin, wickedness" which give a strong tone of Christian condemnation to certain actions of characters in the poem are *synn* and *firen*. For Christian Anglo-Saxons who read the poem, there can be little doubt that the condemnatory tone is there, but the *Beowulf* poet also uses each of these words at least once in the poem with its original, pre-Christian meaning.[87] *Synn* before the conversion meant simply "hostility," and *firen* meant "pain, violence." The *fyrenþearf* suffered by the Danes at the beginning of the poem (14) could not possibly be "sinful need"; it is "painful need"; and the "synn ond sacu" of the Swedish wars (2472) is "hostility and strife," not "sin," just as the "fæhðe ond fyrene" in the same context (2480) would mean "enmity and violence."[88] Having been reminded in these passages of the early, nontheological meaning of these words, the audience would realize when it encountered them in other contexts that, for pre-Christian people like the characters in the poem, the Christian meanings would not have been operative. The Swedes and Geatas of *Beowulf* would have been innocent of the theological dimensions of their violent behavior: what is "wickedness" to the poet's audience was simply pain and strife to them. This contrast of apposed Christian-pagan senses is especially clear in *bealu* and its compounds. Most editors indicate that the central meaning of *bealu* in the poem is "evil." But this is a late signification assigned to the word by Christian reformers of the vocabulary. The primitive sense was "aggression, attack, torment,"[89] and this meaning is dominant in compounds like *bealohycgend* (applied to both Beowulf and the dragon in 2565), *feorhbealu*, *sweordbealu*, and *wigbealu*. Klaeber's glosses like "deadly evil" and "sword evil" for the *-bealu* compounds represent the senses that a perceptive audience of the poem might briefly entertain and then reject as the context in *Beowulf* reminds them of the more relevant pre-Christian senses of *-bealu*. The early sense is especially important when a pagan character uses the word. When Beowulf says, "Ic mid elne sceall / gold gegangan, oððe guð nimeð, / feorhbealu frecne frean eowerne" (2535–37), he is not pronouncing war to be "a deadly evil." The relevant sense is the one suggested by the appositive *guð*—"mortal aggression." Similarly in 2250 *feorhbealu* stands in apposition with *guðdeað*, a precise chias-

56

tic equivalent. *Bealocwealm* in 2265 means "death from attack" (cf. *beaducwealm, wælcwealm); bealu-* here is not, as Klaeber says (p. lxiv, n. 1) "more or less devoid of distinct meaning." Again the poet forces us to assign the word its primitive, concrete meaning in 2826, where the dragon is said to have been "bealwe gebæded"—"pressed by (Beowulf's) attack." If we ignore such reminders as this and the appositives, which constantly emphasize the pre-Christian sense of *bealu*,[90] then we shall impute to the characters in the poem an attitude toward battle and heroic contention which may well have been a part of the Christian world view of poet and audience but which would have been wholly out of keeping with the culture of the men of old in their relentless quest for "dom ær deaðe."

The semantic stratification of Old English poetic diction in Christian times is precisely what the *Beowulf* poet needed to articulate the tensions felt by a people who might say (as Ælfric says in a different context) that they were "of hæðenum magum, æþelborenum swaðeah, of wurðfulre mægðe æfter woruldþingum."[91] These people would find it hard to renounce a heritage as glorious as theirs, even though they acknowledge that it is glorious only "æfter woruldþingum." The *Beowulf* poet's subtle use of apposed word meanings is one means by which he builds a place for the Germanic heroic world in the collective memory of his Christian nation. It is the means also by which he supplies a moving, negative response, as it were, to that simplistic Christian attitude toward ancient pagan heroism stated by Pascal: "Les exemples des morts généreuses de Lacédémoniens et autres ne nous touchent guère. Car qu'est-ce que cela nous apporte? Mais l'exemple de la mort des martyrs nous touche; car ce sont 'nos membres'. Nous avons un lien commun avec eux. . . . Il n'est rien de cela aux exemples des païens: nous n'avons point de liaison à eux."[92]

The author of *Beowulf* is not the only English epic poet who has used the peculiar resources of his native tongue to effect a theological accommodation in his audience's world view. In *Paradise Lost* John Milton exploits dual meanings of words to suggest conflicting perspectives in his account of the Fall of Man. As Arnold Stein, Christopher Ricks, and others have observed,[93] Milton often employs Latin-derived English words with their original Latin word meanings rather than with their conventional English meanings, particularly in parts of the poem devoted to describing Paradise before the Fall. Thus when he describes how dutiful the sun and stars are in shining upon Adam and Eve, Milton does not use the words "dutiful" or "obedient" but rather says that the heavenly bodies are "obsequious" and "officious." In Latin these words carried the innocent meaning "obliging, dutiful," and this is the meaning required by context. But in Milton's English, as in ours today, the words had come to have the pejorative senses "fawning" and "meddlesome." The rivers of Paradise are described as flowing "in mazy error" with "liquid lapse of murm'ring streams," and the reader must supply the Latin meanings "wandering" for "error" and "sliding" or "flowing" for "lapse" (Latin *lapsus*) while remaining aware that, during the time since the words "error" and "lapse" had been borrowed into English, they had developed the negative senses "mistake" and "failing" (cf. "prelapsarian" and "postlapsarian," where "lapse" refers specifically to the Fall of Man). This pattern of bilingual play on words of Latin origin gives the reader a sense of two historical stages in the language Milton is using, a prelapsarian stage when the Latinate words still had their pristine, innocent meanings and a postlapsarian stage when they had developed their pejorative English meanings. Each time he encounters one of these words in Milton's descriptive language, the reader is reminded that he is rooted in postlapsarian time, speaking a fallen language with sullied, vernacular meanings, while for our first parents in Paradise the same words had the pure and wholesome meanings expressive of the paradisal state. Thus, in a psychologically effective way Milton forces the language of his epic to express, through its semantic stratification, a major motif of the poem.

The use of apposed word meanings in *Beowulf* serves the Anglo-Saxon poet's purposes in a similar way. In both cases the poet's language does not merely communicate but rather enacts the meaning of a heroic narrative concerned with man's theological fate. In Milton the polysemous words add poignancy to the poet's backward gaze from postlapsarian time to the happy era before the Fall, while the *Beowulf* poet uses his homonymous diction to suggest the perspective of one gazing back from the time of redemption to the era when men had no hope. But since Milton's device is based upon a more or less accidental linguistic phenomenon (the fact that many seventeenth-century English words happen to have been derived from Latin), it cannot be as intimately cooperative with his poem's theme and perspective as is the *Beowulf* poet's handling of his consistently polysemous diction. By keeping alive, through context and grammatical apposition, both primitive meanings and post-Cædmonian meanings of his traditional poetic language, the *Beowulf* poet forces us to see in the very language of his people living relics of their nation's religious history. Amid the historically determined ambiguities of his Cædmonian formulas, the poet finds a place in his people's mind and language where their ancestors can remain, not with theological security, but with dignity. For, by remaining true to the heroic ideal of *pietas* (or *treowþ*), the men of old came as close as possible to Christian piety; by honoring metod in the primitive sense, they were, unawares, simulating their descendants' faith in Metod in the new, Christian sense. But the poet, in his honesty, never suggests that such simulation, such groping toward true piety, is sufficient for salvation. For that a person must have revelation. A poet cannot save lost souls with poetry, but in the rich imbrications of Old English poetic diction, this poet recognized a powerful emblem of his people's tragic past, and by exploiting these apposed meanings of words in the traditional vocabulary, he was able to vest each line of his poem with deep significance, adding to his celebration of ancestral valor a compassionate tone of Christian regret.

3. GRAMMATICAL APPOSITION
AND SOME BEOWULFIAN THEMES

In the preceding chapters the grammatical term "apposition," after being defined and illustrated, was metaphorically extended to encompass various features of the style of *Beowulf*—apposed elements of compounds, syntactical juxtapositions, significant apposition of scenes, and apposed word meanings. Here I should like to return to the literal grammatical sense of the term and explore some of the ways that apposition functions in *Beowulf*. Apposition of words, phrases, and clauses is so ubiquitous in Old English poetry that scholars have tended to classify it as a standard component of the traditional stylistic apparatus and to consider its function adequately explained by that classification. But in the best poetry inherited components of the traditional style are usually put to work in a way that implements the poet's expressive intentions, and this, in turn, gives freshness and importance to the stylistic devices themselves. This is especially true when frequent use of appositions relating to a particular subject emphasizes a specific theme or subtheme. That is, the apposition lends emphasis to the theme, and the theme, if it is important, gives added emphasis to the appositions through which, in part, it is expressed. This mutually reinforcing process adds accumulatively to our sense of *Beowulf* as an essentially appositional poem in all the senses which have been assigned to that term.

As was noted earlier, apposition, by its very nature, conditions readers to read the poem in a certain way. It is a retarding device and thus forces us to read reflectively, pausing to consider an object or action from more than one perspective as the poet supplies alternate phrasings for the same general referent. It is paratactic and so implies relationships without expressing them, thereby adding to the elliptical quality which is importantly present in the narrative as a whole. Apposition is predominantly nominal and adjectival and thus con-

60

tributes to that sense of stasis in the narrative whereby a state or situation seems to be dwelled on in preference to "a straightforward account of action."[1] Appositions also serve as transitional devices, enabling the poet to move swiftly and easily from one aspect of a subject to another—even within the limits of a single sentence.[2] Beyond these effects, however, apposition functions in various ways to remind the poem's audience of the multiple levels of meaning present in the words that make up the traditional Old English diction as it was adapted by the poet of *Beowulf*.

A very direct means by which apposition calls attention to the polysemy of words is the poet's frequent practice of using an ambiguous word first and then clarifying or narrowing its meaning by a following appositive. Thus near the beginning of the poem the poet says,

> Swa sceal (geong g)uma   gode gewyrcean,
> fromum feohgiftum   on fæder (bea)rme,
> þæt hine on ylde   eft gewunigen
> wilgesiþas,   þonne wig cume,
> leode gelæsten. . . .   [20–24]

A contemporary Christian reader or listener would probably assume that the first long-line by itself means, "Thus must a young man bring about by goodness."[3] But the immediately ensuing appositive "fromum feohgiftum on fæder bearme" drastically narrows the broad meaning of *gode* to the material sense "wealth" or perhaps "generosity with wealth." The audience is forced to revise its Christian sense of the word to a more primitive sense which applies in the pre-Christian world of *Beowulf*, where royal generosity practiced with the expectation of repayment in loyalty was a high virtue in kings. Not every use of these specifying appositions is directly related to this pre-Christian, post-Christian stratification of the vocabulary, but one of the important results of all such appositions is to sensitize the audience's ear to just such stratification.

Minor instances of specifying apposition include:

> þæt se byrnwiga   bugan sceolde,
> feoll on feðan   [2918–19]

and

> þæt he blode fah   bugan sceolde,
> feoll on foldan   [2974–75]

There is a slight suspense in the ambiguity of *bugan,* which could mean either "retreat" (as it does, e.g., in 2956) or "collapse." The appositive formula "feoll on. . ." resolves the ambiguity in each of the passages.

More interesting is the apparent word play on *fah* in 1263–64, where the poet says of Cain, "he þa fag gewat, / morþre gemearcod." The context preceding these verses would have led one to read *fag* as meaning "outlawed, guilty," but the appositive *gemearcod* surprises us by identifying this *fag* as the quite different word meaning "stained, branded." Since both meanings are so appropriate in context, the effect of this apposition is rather to force us to think in terms of double senses than to replace one sense with another.

One instance of this kind of apposition involves a more startling specification of a general term than is usually recognized. Beowulf tells the shore guard that he has heard reports of a monster at Heorot who, on dark nights,

> eaweð þurh egsan   uncuðne nið
> hynðu ond hrafyl   [276–77]

The term "uncuðne nið" is vague: unusual war? unheard-of affliction? strange persecution? The appositive phrase gives shocking clarification, for "hynðu ond hrafyl" would seem to mean "humiliating injury and cannibalism." Scholars seem heretofore to have taken the hapax legomenon *hrafyl* as a compound made up of *hraw* and *fiell* and to mean "the falling of corpses" or, vaguely, "death, slaughter." But the element *fyl* should probably be understood not as a form of *fiell* but rather of *fyll,* "feast, satiety, fill," *hrafyl* meaning "feasting on human bodies," or "cannibalism." The bodies of the Danes whom Grendel had been seizing in Heorot did not, strictly speaking, "fall," but rather the monster snatched them up and gorged on them. (The element *fyll* is used repeatedly in the poem to describe Grendel's grisly feasting on slain victims: cf. lines 125 [*wælfylle*], 734 [*wistfylle*], and 1333 [*fylle*].) It is this characteristic that makes his attacks so "strange" (*uncuð*) and, to a people given to reverent burial customs, an abasement (*hynðu*).

It is unnecessary to discuss in detail all the specifying variations, but it may be well to list a few of them briefly to give some sense of their pervasiveness in the poem:

wræc micel [a great exile? vengeance? misery?] . . . modes brecða [misery] [170–71]

flota [seaman? crew? ship?] . . . bat [ship] [210–11; cf. 294–95]

wlite [ornamental trappings? appearance, countenance?] . . . ænlic ansyn [appearance, countenance] [250–51][4]

swæsne eþel [ancestral property? native land? realm?] . . . lond Brondinga, / . . . þær he folc ahte, /burh ond beagas [the realm *is* his ancestral property] [520–22][5]

heardra nan [no brave warriors? no hard weapons?] . . . iren ærgod [hard weapons] [988]

guðwerigne [battle weary? dead?] . . . aldorleasne [dead] [1586–87]

mid gewealdum [powerfully? on purpose?] . . . sylfes willum [on purpose] [2221–22]

eormenlafe æðelan cynnes [mighty remnant of a noble race (i.e., a human survivor)? immense legacy of a noble race?] . . . deore maðmas [immense legacy] [2234–36]

mægenes [strength? virtue? an armed force?] . . . godra guðrinca [an armed force] [2647–48]

Some of the clarifying appositions simply explain metaphors: "hildeleoman . . . billa selest" (1143–44), "bitan . . . aldre sceþðan" (1524–25), "weard . . . sawele hyrde" (1741–42), "biteran stræle . . . wom wundorbebodum" (1746–47), "merehrægla . . . segl" (1905–6), "woruldcandel . . . sigel" (1965–66), "hiorodryncum swealt . . . bille gebeaten" (2358–59). It is possible that in 2955–56, where we are told that Ongentheow mistrusted his ability "heaðoliðendum hord forstandan, / bearn ond bryde," *hord* is a metaphor which is explained by "bearn ond bryde"—that is, his "treasures" are his wife and children.[6] But the usual reading of "hord . . . bearn ond bryde" as enumeration rather than apposition is possible too.

The poet also uses apposition as a means of reinstating the primitive, concrete meaning of the traditional compounds and phrases of Old English poetic diction. Since the element *hilde-* is so common in Old English poetry, there is danger that when the poet says *hildegrap* in 1446, it will be perceived by a semiattentive ear as no more than a metrically motivated synonym for *grap*. To prevent this misreading, he supplies the appositive "eorres inwitfeng"— "anger's malicious grip." This association brings vividly alive the elemental meaning of both components in *hildegrap*. Elsewhere he uses "grip" terms metaphorically, as when Beowulf exultantly describes how pain holds Grendel in a tight grasp: "ac hyne sar hafað / in nidgripe nearwe befongen, / balwon bendum" (975–77). Here *balwon* reinforces the sense of *nid; bendum* reinforces *gripe*, and the intervening modifier "nearwe befongen" brings out yet more strongly the sense of a pinching, painful grip. There is good reason for the poet's concern to emphasize the concrete aspects of this image of gripping. The use of words like *gripe* and *bend* in metaphorical expressions was so cliché in Old English poetry that audiences must often have disregarded their literal meanings. Poets spoke of the grip of stones (*Elene* 824, *Solomon and Saturn* 76), of spears (*Andreas* 187), of wild beasts (*Juliana* 125), and of flames (*Juliana* 391, *Elene* 1302). Similarly *bend* is used with some frequency in connection with pain (*witebend* in *Andreas* 108) or death (*deaðes bend* in *Christ* 1042; and cf. *Beowulf* 1007, 2901, 3045). Therefore, if the audience is to perceive the metaphor in these conventional expressions, the poet must do something to revive their figurative content. It is particularly important that he do so in describing Grendel in the grip of pain, for there the figure of speech creates an ironic reference which gives rhetorical force to Beowulf's speech. Before the passage in question, he has just lamented his failure to hold Grendel, to bind him in hard clamps ("heardan clammum . . . wriþan"), to requite him with his handgrip (*mundgripe*). Nonetheless, he reassures Hrothgar, the monster is now in the (metaphorical) grip of pain, which will hold him until metod decides his fate.[7]

The device of using appositives which "translate" the elements of a foregoing phrase or compound can freshen the sense of poetic formulas in various ways. In 2328, for example, the compound *hygesorga* might be mistaken for a mere alliterative variant of *sorga*, were it not that "hygesorga mæst" stands in apposition to "hreow on hreðre," which forces attention to the sense "heart's distress, distress of spirit." This effect in turn is preparatory for the image in 2331–32, "breost innan weoll / þeostrum geþoncum." The first occurrence of the compound *eorðsele* is accompanied by the appositive "hlæw under hrusan," which not only calls attention to the component parts of *eorðsele* but also specifies how they relate to each other: "a chamber under the ground." (Without this clarification, we might analyze *eorðsele* on the model of *eorðweall* and misinterpret the word as "a chamber made of earth.") In 1972–73 Beowulf is described as "wigendra hleo," a phrase followed by the appositive *lindgestealla*. Here the semantically analogous elements *hleo* and *lind-* reinforce each other. If *lind-* did not follow, *hleo* could be taken in the sense of "lord" rather than the original sense of "protector, shelter." In return, *hleo,* thus clarified, assures that *lindgestealla* will be understood not in the most obvious sense of "warrior with a shield" but rather as "comrade who is a shield" or "shielding comrade." The compound *modsefa* is common in poetry (the Bessinger-Smith concordance records forty-four occurrences) and is usually designated a "tautological compound." When it appears in 349, however, the poet adds the appositive "wig ond wisdom" in the line following. This appositive activates a nontautological sense in *modsefa, mod-* meaning "courage" (as in *modþracu,* 385) and *sefa* corresponding to *wisdom,* understanding." In all subsequent occurrences of *modsefa* (1853, 2012, 2628), a meaning for the compound which combined the senses "wisdom" and "courage" ("sapientia et fortitudo") would not be inappropriate.[8] "Valor-mindedness" or, less awkwardly, "valiant spirit," may suggest the meaning which the *Beowulf* poet was assigning the word.

If we are willing to acknowledge this pattern of appositions in which the elements of the locutions standing in apposition are in more or less symmetrical relation to each other, then perhaps we should reconsider C.L. Wrenn's suggestion that the manuscript reading of *Beowulf* 466–67 is defensible:

    ond on geogoðe heold   gimme rice
    hordburh hæleþa

Most editors emend to "ginne rice" ("spacious kingdom"), but to do so destroys the semantic symmetry of "gimme rice," "jewel kingdom," and *hordburh,* "treasure city." Von Schaubert, citing Ekwall, dismisses Wrenn's proposal of a compound *gimmerice* because Wrenn gave no satisfactory explanation as to why *gimm* should appear in the compound as *gimme.* But *gimme* need not be a compound element. Since final *-a* in the *Beowulf* manuscript sometimes appears as *-e*,[9] *gimme* could be a late spelling of *gimma*, genitive plural, and the apposition in question could mean "the realm of jewels, the stronghold of treasure."

What is especially worthy of notice in these symmetrical and other appositions which function to emphasize or revivify meanings of traditional compounds and formulas[10] is that they exercise the audience's mind in noticing elemental meanings of words or in recalling etymological origins. This is an exercise required elsewhere in the poem as well, where the poet uses a word in a context which forces recognition of the original sense of the term. In 1284–87, for example, we are told that the battle strength of Grendel's dam is less than that of Grendel by as much as a female's strength is less than a male's. The word used for male is *wæpnedman,* a word common to prose as well as poetry and meaning "the male of the species." Lest the audience forget that the term is made up of words originally meaning "person with a weapon,"[11] the poet provides the following context for *wæpnedmen:*

                       be wæpnedmen
    þonne heoru bunden,   hamere geþruen,
    sweord swate fah   swin ofer helme
    ecgum dyhtig   andweard scireð

Grendel did not use weapons, of course, but for the sake of heightening the contrast between the fearfulness of a man's strength in combat and that of a woman, the poet "etymologizes" *wæpnedmen* and develops from the etymology the vignette of a man wielding fierce weapons in battle.

The word *maðelian,* which, starting in 286, is used so frequently in *Beowulf,* did not mean simply "speak" but meant rather "speak formally." The original sense was "to make a speech in the presence of an assembled group," the verb being formed from *mæðel,* "meeting, assembly of people."[12] The exact primitive sense of the Old English verb is captured in the Harley Glossary entry containing "contestatur in populo . maðelaþ."[13] Fifty lines before the poet's first use of the *maðelode* formula he employs another device for semantically rejuvenating *maðelian* when he introduces a speech with a phrase which is in effect an etymological analysis of *maðelian.* The shore guard, he says, "meþelwordum frægn"—"inquired using words appropriate to the mæðel." Having called attention here to "mæðel-words," his ensuing uses of maðelian will be more likely to strike the ear with full etymological force. In two places he seems to remind us of the fact that the verb means "to speak before an assembly": "Wealhðeo maþelode, heo fore þæm werede spræc" (1215) and "Wiglaf maðelode, wordrihta fela / sægde gesiðum" (2631–32). These contexts, once more, seem to return the word to its sense of "contestatur in populo."

The poetic words oretta and oretmæcg are used fairly commonly in Old English poetry, apparently as loose synonyms for "champion, warrior." In origin, however, the element oret- had a very specific meaning. Its earlier form was *or-hat, which displays its relation to Old English (ge)hat "vow, promise" and hatan "to vow, promise, call." Taking into account the intensive prefix or-, we might assume that the literal, primitive meaning of oretmæcg would have been something like "man of the ultimate (or primal) vow." The Beowulf poet is probably taking cognizance of the early sense of the word when he says (480–81): "Ful oft gebeotedon beore druncne / ofer ealowæge oretmecgas." Using the compound here as the subject of the verb gebeotedon (itself derived from the same root word, -hat [beot < *bihat]), meaning "vowed," the poet restores to the word some of its primitive force. Since a vow (especially an "ultimate vow") is easily taken as a threat, and since vows warriors make are (as in Beowulf 480–81) usually vows to wage battle, oretmæcg and oretta take on a somewhat combative tone, implying "challenger" or something comparably pugnacious. Thus Beowulf and his men are described as oretmecgas when they march heavily armed into the land of the Danes without having asked permission of the Danish authorities (332; cf. 244–47). Caroline Brady has shown how all the occurrences of oretta and oretmæcg in Beowulf seem to imply an awareness by the poet of the root meaning of oret-, and this is particularly true of the last appearance of an oret- word in 2538, where Beowulf is called "rof oretta" just after he utters his vow to defeat the dragon or die.[14]

These instances in which the poet uses context and the ubiquitous appositions to revive earlier senses of words are probably part of his larger intentions in Beowulf. In the preceding chapter it was noted that the poet systematically exploits the semantic layering of Old

English poetic vocabulary, rejuvenating pre-Christian meanings of theological words while simultaneously keeping the postconversion senses operative. Our examination of the appositions in this chapter thus far suggests that not only the theological terms but the vocabulary at large is constantly probed for earlier senses of words, primarily through the use of apposition but also through other manipulations of context. Through these stylistic strategies we are reminded from first to last that the poet's traditional language is fraught with history, and it is within the historical layers of word meanings that the poet expresses one of his most important themes.

But the appositions work in other ways as well to serve thematic ends. Certain objects described in the poem are emphasized and are given special significance through the use of appositions. An example is the boar image, which was cited in the first chapter as one of many traditional Germanic trappings which the poet mentions throughout the poem to place the action subtly but firmly in pre-Christian time. The boar was a totemic animal associated in the North with Frea. To it were ascribed supernatural powers of protection over warriors in battle.[15] Helmets surviving from Anglo-Saxon England show boar shapes cast into metal strips used to reinforce the crowns of these headpieces. But would the heathen properties of the boar image survive in memory throughout the Anglo-Saxon period? Perhaps not, and therefore the *Beowulf* poet has used appositions to highlight these early meanings of the boar in Germanic society and at the same time to develop a motif which supplements the Christian-pagan theme.

The first mention of the boar image is in 303–6:

> Eoforlic scionon
> ofer hleorber[g]an   gehroden golde,
> fah ond fyrheard,—   ferhwearde heold
> guþmod grímmon.[16]

The first clause (down to the hyphen) is literal description. The second clause is an appositive restatement in terms which suggest the supernatural potency of the images: the boar, which is personified (see *guþmod*), extends protective power over the lives of the warriors. Of course the metal effigies on Anglo-Saxon helmets did give physical protection to the skull inside the helmet by their reinforcing effect, but something more than structural bracing seems implied here,[17]

and later in the poem the boar's supernatural properties are made
explicit in appositions. Thus Beowulf's helmet is described as

befongen freawrasnum,   swa hine fyrndagum
worhte wæpna smið,   wundrum teode,
besette swinlicum,   þæt hine syðþan no
brond ne beadomecas   bitan ne meahton.   [1451–54]

That is, "encompassed with lordly bands, as the smith fashioned it in
ancient days, provided with supernatural powers, set about with
boar images." Since *wundrum* specifies supernatural powers, and
since the boar was the animal associated with Freyr in Scandinavian
mythology, it is tempting to see in the unique compound *freawrasnum* an allusion to an Anglo-Saxon god Frea (cognate with Freyja,
the Old Icelandic deity). But such an explicit naming of the pagan
god seems unlikely; it is more probable that the word meant "lord,"
and there is present here that carefully maintained double sense seen
elsewhere in *Beowulf* where a word which had in earlier times been
applied to pagan gods and was in Christian times transferred to the
Christian deity is used with calculated ambiguity in the context of the
world of *Beowulf*.[18]

Remembering the supernatural status of the boar image, we may
be able to understand a long-disputed word in another of the appositions dealing with the boar symbol. In *Beowulf* 2152 we are told that
Hrothgar gave to Beowulf an "eafor, heafodsegn." *Eafor* is usually
taken to refer to a battle standard or some other war gear with a boar
figure on it, with *heafodsegn* serving as an appositional restatement
of *eafor*. But the compound is puzzling, as Klaeber's note on the line
(p. 206) suggests: "Was it called a 'head sign' because it was borne
aloft in front of the king? . . . Or does the compound mean 'great
banner'? Or, perhaps, an emblem (boar) such as was attached to the
helmet which covered the head?" The word *heafodsegn* occurs no-
where else, but there are numerous other English compounds in
which *heafod* as first element means "major, of special importance."
Thus *cwide* means "saying," but *heafodcwide* means "a saying of
special importance"; *stede* means "place," but *heafodstede* means
"an exalted or sacred place"; *mægen* means "virtue," but *heafod-
mægen* means "cardinal virtue"; *leahter* means "sin," but *heafod-
leahter* means "mortal sin." From this pattern we may infer that
heafodsegn would mean "a sign of special importance." If so, then

this apposition is like the one just discussed; a term for "boar" or "boar image" stands with an appositive which designates the exceptional status of the boar symbol.[19]

If we are correct in assuming that these appositions are reminders of the protective power which pagan Germanic people attributed to the boar images, then it is easy to see why the poet gives appositional emphasis to the boar images on the helmets when he describes the pyre at Finnsburg (1110–13):

Æt þæm ade wæs   eþgesyne
swatfah syrce,   swyn ealgylden,
eofer irenheard,   æþeling manig
wundum awyrded;   sume on wæle crungon!

Here the vaunted power of the boar to protect warriors is exposed for what it is worth. And a few lines later the poet may have intended one final sardonic allusion to the pagans' trust in protective boar helmets when he says, "hafelan multon" (1120).[20]

The use of apposition in developing the boar image into an epitome of the tragic delusions of the heroic society of *Beowulf* illustrates in a specific way how this syntactical device can serve thematic concerns. But the appositions dealing with the boar are but a fraction of a much larger number of appositions dealing with a variety of inanimate objects in the poem.[21] The nominal compounds similarly suggest that "the *Beowulf* poet is predominantly interested in riches and ornaments (39 compounds) and in . . . compounds referring to the banqueting hall and . . . to the drinking goblet. . . . It is therefore the artificial, man-made aspect of the visible world which holds his attention, and in comparison with these the compounds referring to nature are few in number."[22] And Klaeber similarly comments on the large number of "epithets exhibiting the ancient pride in skill of workmanship" (p. 137). Does this proliferation of appositions and compounds (most of them introduced through appositions) referring to man-made objects serve, like the boar references, the thematic concerns of the poet? It certainly bespeaks a preoccupation with the artificial over the natural which strikes the modern reader as peculiar.

In order to understand this predilection suggested by the poet's distribution of appositions and compounds, it will be necessary to recall in some detail the difference between medieval and modern attitudes toward the natural world and the world of man's artifice. For the modern man or woman schooled in Rousseau and Wordsworth, it is sometimes hard to realize that nature was not always regarded as the beneficent entity envisioned by the Romantics. Early medieval Christians knew that God cursed the earth after the Fall (Genesis 3:17–19).[23] The Old English poems *Genesis* A 930–1001 and *Genesis* B 802–15 vividly record this frightening moment in human history, and the Old English translator of Orosius too, in an addition to his original's account of how the earth is punished for men's sins, reminds us that when Adam fell, God visited manifold afflictions upon the earth and reduced its fruitfulness.[24] Later in the Anglo-Saxon period Ælfric sums up the facts about nature's fundamental hostility toward mankind.[25] After the Fall, says Ælfric, cold, hunger, and disease came into the world. Dragons, serpents, and wild animals that had previously not dared to molest mankind became dangerous and implacable foes. Even the elements fire and water, which had previously been only sources of comfort, begin to present mortal danger to people on earth. In this new and fallen world man must struggle against the hostilities and temptations of nature and exert diligent efforts to preserve such God-given virtues and customs as remained to him. It is discipline and rational organization that offer the best hedges against a malevolent nature. Or, as Isidore argues in his *Synonyma*,[26] it is Reason to which man should turn, a view shared by Boethius and his Anglo-Saxon translator.[27]

Where nature is malevolent and chaotic, artifice is reassuring, and this, I believe, explains the remarkable accumulation of appositions and compounds for man-made, as opposed to natural, things in *Beowulf*. The man-made wall, the road, the ship, the hall, and human clothing and armor are not only practically useful but also are comforting symbols of the ability of man, through skill and reason, to subdue and control the natural world. It is not surprising that, in addition to real property, smaller possessions like cups, helmets, coats of mail, and weapons are carefully disposed of in Anglo-Saxon wills.[28] Moreover, in literary records of the period there is "constant reference to precious objects."[29] Perhaps most revealing is the fact that the precious objects and even objects of daily use were often covered with the artistic designs so distinctive of the Anglo-Saxons. Whitelock has described the design well, although with a curiously disparaging tone: "The commonest decoration is the Germanic zoomorphic style, which, long before the Anglo-Saxons used it, had lost all naturalistic intention and become a mere pattern formed by distorted animal or bird forms, or even by detached parts of such forms, heads or limbs arranged as mere elements in a design."[30] I suspect that "mere pattern" would have struck an Anglo-Saxon as an oddly condescending phrase. It is precisely the reduction of natural animal forms to pattern that gave pleasure and reassurance to those who created and those who enjoyed the Germanic zoomorphic style: seeing forms from the natural world forced into abstract designs and geometric symmetries reminds one that the hand and mind of man can control the menacing forces of nature. Whether working in metal, stone, or manuscript illumination, the Anglo-Saxon artist delighted to see birds, snakes, and quadrupeds as well as dragons and other fabulous beasts subdued, constrained, and even dismembered for the sake of an aesthetically pleasing design, just as in *Beowulf* sea creatures, dragons, and trolls are subdued when they threaten man and his artifacts. Perhaps it is in manuscript illumination that the social symbolism is most complete: beasts, denaturalized and often dismembered, are made to assume symmetrical, angular shapes which form a letter of the alphabet, which completes a word, which expresses a human thought. But all forms of art must have been comforting to an Anglo-Saxon: every scribble and design on a brooch, byrnie, or drinking horn is a triumph of the ordering intellect over disordered, anarchic nature.

In the story of Beowulf we see a similar opposition of artifice and nature. The hall Heorot, whose construction receives such mythopoeic emphasis, is a bastion of order and safety which throws light into the surrounding darkness (309–11). Beyond Heorot, its adjacent *buras,* and their protective *weall* lie the forest, the fens, and the mere, swarming with reptilian and monstrous life. The story of the Grendelkin is the story of the invasion of the citadel—the place of light and order—by the creature from the vernal shade who strives against human order.

> Swa rixode ond wið rihte wan,
> ana wið eallum, oðþæt idel stod
> husa selest. [144–46]

Beowulf frees the artifact of Heorot from Grendel's hold and returns the wise creator of the hall to power. Similarly, at the end of the poem Beowulf wrests from the dragon's hold the artifacts in the treasure hoard and returns them to the possession of men.

In a poem such as this, it is to be expected that artifacts will assume a special importance and that the poet's style will reflect that importance. In 1441–54 and 1502–12, for example, Beowulf's armor is given extraordinary attention as he descends into the mere, making his deepest penetration into the alien world of nature. Not only the appositions and compounds, but personifications as well highlight the hero's byrnie and helmet.[31] The mailcoat woven by men's hands "knew how" to protect Beowulf's body (1443–45); the shining helmet, exalted with treasure, had to "seek out" the swirling depths (1448–50). His sword too is humanized: it sings a battle lay, is greedy but will not bite, and thereby loses *dom* (1521–28). We are reminded of the pervasive identifications of men with artifacts through metaphor: a king is *eodor, helm,* and *hleo;*[32] a sword is a *guðwine,* and a *secg* can be either a man or a sword, just as *heard* can modify both a man and a weapon. The climax of the fight with Grendel's mother makes overt the importance of this stylistic emphasis on artifacts as allies of men and the forces of good. The murderous ogress is foiled by the woven mailcoat, and we are told that God, through the byrnie, gave victory to the hero (1547–54). Beowulf's subsequent decapitation of Grendel's corpse with a sword demonstrates that the monster's immunity to weapons (which the poet significantly refers to as *goda* in 681) has been broken. No longer are artifacts nullified by nature's monstrous forces.[33] So prominent in this episode is the opposition between man-made armor and menacing nature (the water, the sea beasts, the darkness, and the monster herself) that the designation of Beowulf here as "hringa þengel" (1507) seems likely to refer to his ring-mail armor rather than to gold rings, as Klaeber (p. 360) thinks.[34] The same systematic antithesis of man-made armor and hostile nature emphasized through appositions, is found in 549–53: "Wæs merefixa mod onhrered; / þær me wið laðum licsyrce min / heard hondlocen helpe gefremede, / beadohrægl broden, on breostum læg / golde gegyrwed."

Cunningly made armor and ornaments, well-wrought buildings, damascened swords, treasure-decked saddles and bridles (which control the stallion's power for the use of men), and artfully curved ships deserve the emphasis they receive through apposition and epithet simply because they are artificial, not natural. And the apparent absence of stylistic emphasis on the opposing forces of nature is because it is the monsters, who are abundantly present in the poem's appositions and compounds, who, for the most part, represent nature. The human essence is to be found in the artificial, and the works of men's hands not only express but actually help implement their desire for rational control. In a remarkable sentence in lines 320–21, we are told that "stræt wæs stanfah, stig wisode / gumum ætgæ-dere." The road which men have laid across the wilderness and adorned with bright, ornamental stones becomes, as it were, the tutor of men, guiding them to where they should go. Where other cultures have preferred *naturam sequi,* the poet of *Beowulf* seems to say, "follow the example of your artifacts—be guided by human reason and control." And they *are* so guided, the customs and rituals men form to order human nature being celebrated no less than the material objects they fashion as they express their control over external nature. "Cuþe he duguðe þeaw," says the poet (359), and there is that same pleasure in the patterned behavior of the man that there is in patterned artifacts. References to the details of Germanic law (e.g., in 73, 2608, 2886) assume added significance in the light of this theme, and the pathetic allusions to Grendel's indifference to the rules of wergild (especially in 154–58) are not, I believe, "toyed with almost humorously"[35] but rather are serious expressions of the conflict between anarchic nature and the world of human order. Without custom, law, and ritual, man finds himself in the state of nature, where, in Hobbes's famous formulation, there is only "continuall feare, and danger of violent death; and the life of man, solitary, poore, nasty, brutish, and short."[36]

One of the most elaborately patterned rituals in *Beowulf* is that of the banquet, whose stately forms are repeated and alluded to throughout the poem. The seating of the guest (e.g., 489–90, 1785–86, 1977–78, 2011–13), the passing of the cup (615–24, 1169–1231, 1980–83, 2020–24), gift giving (1020–49, 1192–1220, 1866–69, 2101–3, 2142–47, 2152–66, 2172–76, 2190–96), and the retirement of the king (644–46, 1790–92) all recur in predictable sequence again and again, making the banquet scene almost a choreographed spectacle.[37] But these rituals are not merely ostentatious. In them we see confirmation of the king's sovereignty and constant reaffirmation of the mutual loyalties felt by thanes toward their lord and toward one another. And, of course, the rituals enact man's reassuring ability to impose pattern and control on his own behavior. By giving ritual and symbolism to the animal function of ingesting food and drink, man differentiates himself from creatures in the state of nature. It is not surprising that the wretched exile in *The Wanderer* recalls the banqueting scene with such agonized regret or that in *Beowulf* the only characters who take food without ritual are the monstrous Grendelkin.

The pattern and meaning resident in one aspect of the banqueting ritual has been insufficiently recognized, and as a result, several passages in *Beowulf* have been imperfectly understood. It is well known that the thanes' acceptance of the king's hospitality and gifts is a physical acknowledgment of their fealty to him. "Ic him þa maðmas, þe he me sealde, / geald æt guðe," says Beowulf (2490–91), stating in clearest possible terms the contractual importance of accepting royal generosity. The banquet was one of the most public forms of ritual exchange. "In clan society, eating and drinking were a symbol and a confirmation of mutual social obligations."[38] The drinking rituals are especially important, if we can trust the evidence of the many compounds in *Beowulf* formed on *meodu-, ealu-, beor-,* and *win-.* Modern readers, to whom drinking seems more often a social problem than a social ritual, are apt to miss the significance of serving the cup to men.

We know from *The Fight at Finnsburg* that warriors who drink from the king's cup in the meadhall were expected, when war broke out, to repay his generosity with loyal valor: "Ne gefrægn ic næfre . . . / swanas hwitne medo sel forgyldan, / ðonne Hnæfe guldan his hægstealdas" (37–40).[39] We know from *Maldon* and from *Beowulf* itself that the vow to serve the leader was made when the warrior drank the mead, as if accepting the drink confirmed the binding force of the oath:

Gemunu þa mæla   þe we oft æt meodo spræcon,
þonne we on bence   beot ahofon,
hæleð on healle,   ymbe heard gewinn;
nu mæg cunnian   hwa cene sy.   [*Maldon* 211–15][40]

Ic ðæt mæl geman, þær we medu þegun,
þonne we geheton ussum hlaforde
in biorsele, ðe us ðas beagas geaf,
þæt we him ða guðgetawa gyldan woldon,
gif him þyslicu þearf gelumpe,
helmas ond heard sweord.   [*Beowulf* 2633–38]

Snorri Sturlusson describes the ritual of the oath cup (*bragarful*) in
Ynglinga saga, and it is tempting to see implicit in the *Beowulfian*
banquets some of the details specified in the Icelander's circumstan-
tial account. Snorri says that the person to whom the cup is brought
must "stand up, take the *Brage*-beaker, make solemn vows to be
afterward fulfilled, and thereupon empty the beaker." He then illustrates how even a king is bound by vows made at the drinking ritual:
"When the full Brage-beaker came in, King Ingjald stood up, grasped
a large bull's horn, and made a solemn vow to enlarge his dominion
by one half, towards all the four corners of the world, or die; and
thereupon he emptied the beaker at a single draft."[41] There are
allusions to this ritual elsewhere in sagas and poetry,[42] and it is
difficult not to see suggestions of it in *Beowulf.* The hero stands to
drink, apparently, when he is presented with the cup in Heorot:
"Beowulf geþah / ful on flette" (1024–25), and Klaeber observes
that his behavior is "no doubt in obedience to well-regulated courtly
custom" (p. 169).[43] When Wealhtheow first brings the cup to
Beowulf, he ceremonially accepts it and then makes his formal vow
to save her people from Grendel or die in the attempt (628–38). The
solemnity of vows made while drinking is underlined in Saxo Gram-
maticus's version of Hjalto's speech in *Bjarkamál:* "We perform with
brave hearts everything that we uttered with mouths that had drunk
from the cup, and we fulfill the vows we swore by highest Jove and
the powers above."[44] Apparently the vow uttered while drinking
from the lord's cup is an oath made before the gods.

It is important to keep this in mind when we read Hrothgar's
account of how his thanes had vowed to fight his enemy Grendel
(480–88):

Ful oft gebeotedon beore druncne
ofer ealowæge oretmecgas,
þæt hie in beorsele bidan woldon
Grendles guþe mid gryrum ecga.
Ðonne wæs þeos medoheal on morgentid,

drihtsele dreorfah,   þonne dæg lixte,
eal bencþelu   blode bestymed,
heall heorudreore;   ahte ic holdra þy læs,
deorre duguðe,   þe þa deað fornam.

Here the collocation of *gebeotedon* and *oretmecgas* with "beore druncne" and "ofer ealowæge" makes clear that this is the ritual vow sworn over the drinking cup. Having drunk the beer, the vow swearers (*oretmecgas*) uttered their vow that they would face Grendel. The phrase "beore druncne" in line 480 is to be understood as "having drunk the [lord's] beer," just as in *Andreas* 1003 "dreore druncne" means "having drunk blood." To translate *druncne* as "drunk, inebriated" is logically impossible in the *Andreas* passage and inappropriate in *Beowulf* 480. And yet this is precisely how scholars have rendered the phrase in translation and glossary, representing Hrothgar as contemptuously calling his warriors "drunk with beer,"[45] "made bold with beer,"[46] or "drunken with beer."[47] But there is no insinuation by the king that his thanes are mere "pot-valiant men" (as David Wright's translation has it). The appositive epithets he applies to them—"holdra . . . deorre duguðe"—show with what affection and respect he is referring to his retinue. They are "faithful" and "dear," for they swore loyally to do battle with his monstrous adversary and then gave their lives in an effort to carry out that vow. Overlooking the significance of drinking while uttering a vow, we have misread as an inappropriate, unmotivated sneer a speech whose only tone is one of gratitude, admiration, and bereavement.

Even more problematic is the conclusion of Wealhtheow's speech in 1228–31. After thanking Beowulf for having achieved what she and her people requested of him, she repeatedly asks that he support her royal sons. Then, as is her wont, she adds anxious public assurances that the Danish retinue around her (including, no doubt, Hrothulf) will prove loyal to prince and comrade and eager to obey the royal will:

Her is æghwylc eorl   oþrum getrywe,
modes milde,   mandrihtne hol[d],
þegnas syndon geþwære,   þeod ealgearo,
druncne dryhtguman   doð swa ic bidde.

As in the previous passage, here appositions emphasize the motif of warriors who have drunk the king's mead being *hold* "loyal" and *geþwære* "obedient" to their *mandrihten* and to their queen. But again modern attitudes toward drinking have obscured the intended interrelation between the appositions in the sentence, leading some scholars to see sarcasm and irony where it is least appropriate. Thus Hoops's gloss:

> **druncne dryhtguman dōð swā ic bidde** "die trunknen Gefolgsmannen tun, wie (was) ich sie bitte". Dies scheint in der Tat der Gipfel der Ironie.[48]

Wrenn is representative of many scholars in his attempt to soften Hoops's harsh interpretation of *druncne* as "trunknen," observing, "**druncne**. Here the past part. implies only that the retainers were mellowed with their drinking."[49] In addition to "mellowed," translators have offered the delicate renderings "cheered with drink," "flown with drink," "reveling," "wine-cheered," "wine-glad," and "wine-joyous." But Wrenn was on a better track when he added to his note that *druncne* "could almost be rendered as an active perf. part., 'having drunk.' " The implication is that not only are the warriors *getrywe*, *hold*, and *geþwære*, but they have even confirmed their devotion to the rulers by drinking the royal mead.[50] The logic of Wealhtheow's association of loose appositives may be suggested by paraphrase: "Here every nobleman is loyal to his king, the thanes are obedient, the nation in complete readiness: having drunk [the royal mead], the retainers will [surely] do as I ask." In the next line but one, the poet says "druncon win weras," suggesting that the warriors respond to her words with formal affirmation of their readiness to serve their royal benefactors. There is the usual anxiety in Wealhtheow's speech, but no irony—except for the tragic irony apparent to an audience that knows what Hrothulf will do in future years.

Perhaps other passages in *Beowulf* where drinking is mentioned should also be reassessed. When we are told that the hero "nealles druncne slog / heorðgeneatas" (2179–80), we should probably understand that King Beowulf, unlike Heremod, had not struck his companions of the hearth who had accepted his drink (and thus, by implication, sworn loyalty to him). A reader is naive who mistakes the sense as "he did not strike his retainers, even when they were drunk." This would be a curious emphasis in context.

I hesitate to suggest a revisionary reading of Beowulf's retort to

Unferth ("Hwæt, þu worn fela, wine min *Unferth*, / beore druncen ymb Brecan spræce" [530–31]), so accustomed are we to savoring a barbed insinuation that Unferth is talking in his cups. But even here the hero may be implying that Unferth's flaw is more than just overdrinking. One versed in the rituals of meadhall vows might well infer a different kind of insult in Beowulf's words: "Having drunk your lord's mead, Unferth, you do not make the expected *gilpcwide* pledging to defend your benefactor, but instead you babble about Breca and his deeds." In the context of their hostile exchange this implication may have seemed even more stinging than a hint at intoxication.[51] This is not to say, however, that drunkeness carried no stigma. We know from other Old English texts—especially penitentials and homilies—that overindulging in drink, and especially encouraging guests to overindulge, were condemned. But if the audience of *Beowulf* felt contempt for the drinking at Hrothgar's and Hygelac's banquets, they would probably have realized that their contempt resulted from their Christian training, while in that earlier, more innocent time described in the poem, drinking the king's mead had a different social function and different implications. The drinking ritual, like so much else in the life and language of the poem, is one of those heroic-age motifs that distance the audience from the world of their forebears even as it recalls sympathetically the ways of that bygone era. Judged by Christian standards, the heroes were misguided and lost; but they were "æghwæs untæle ealde wisan": "in every way blameless according to the ancient way" (1865).

We should notice that although motifs like the old drinking vows, the portentous boar images, and the inimical character of nature can be found overtly stated in Germanic tradition, in *Beowulf* the signification of these motifs is conveyed largely through suggestive collocation. Words referring to vows occur next to words referring to drink; terms for boar images appear in apposition with words like *wundor* denoting supernatural power; and references to nature seem to cluster more around descriptions of monsters than of men, while the latter are loosely associated with artifacts. Like many of the most important meanings in the poem, these must be inferred from juxtapositions and loose associations, and throughout *Beowulf*, readers' minds are conditioned to make just such inferences. For constantly at work in the poem's style, exercizing the readers' im-

agination in drawing conclusions from verbal collocations and juxtapositions, are the appositional devices which have formed the
subject of these lectures. Whether seen in the narrow context of
grammatical apposition, or in the larger context of appositive style in
general, this literary device or habit of mind is subtly yet powerfully
present in *Beowulf* at every level, serving the expressive needs of a
theme which by its very nature must emerge more through suggestion than through assertion. Of the two terms just used, "habit of
mind" is perhaps preferable to "literary device," for apposition
works at a more elemental level of expression than does a "device." It
occupies a middle ground between grammar and style, between
syntax and narrative method. Appositions and appositive style are
the automatic means by which an Old English poet proceeds from
thought to thought. They can be simultaneously transitional, nomi-
nalizing and emphasizing as they bring out by suggestion the complex meanings of events, motifs, and words. Their most important
function, perhaps, is their role in focusing attention on the homony-
mic character of Old English poetic diction, for this serves most
pervasively the expression of pagan-Christian tensions which concern the poet so deeply. It is the combining of this concern and the
appositional style that enables the poet to release the power of his
inherited diction in a way unmatched in any other Anglo-Saxon
poem. The expressive potential of Old English appositive style would
have been hard to imagine, had *Beowulf* not revealed it, and con-
versely it would be hard to imagine the poem *Beowulf* apart from its
appositive style. In reading *Beowulf,* as in reading all great poetry, we
have the sense that the author's genius has been happily merged with
the one style and language which alone could convey his poetic
apprehension of his subject.

Just as in the first chapter I undertook a close scrutiny of the opening
sentence of *Beowulf,* I shall close with a brief analysis of the final
sentence, and especially of the apposed epithets with which the poem
ends:

> cwædon þæt he wære   wyruldcyning[a]
> mannum mildust   ond mon(ðw)ærust,
> leodum liðost   ond lofgeornost.   [3180–82][52]

The closing sequence of appositions, consisting of a series of balanced superlatives, has sometimes puzzled students of the poem. Why, after 3,000 lines describing the physical strength, the fierce courage, and the astounding feats of Beowulf, does the poet conclude his narrative by emphasizing the hero's gentleness and kindness? That Beowulf did have these qualities is apparent to the careful reader of the poem: his protective attitude toward Wealhtheow's sons, his concern for the well-being of his own companions,[53] his magnanimous treatment of Unferth, his tender affection for Hygelac, and his refusal of the throne in favor of Heardred all bespeak a kind and even gentle side of his stern character. But we must search rather diligently among the long and ringing accounts of his prowess, his boasts, and his triumphs, and his proud fulfillment of his *heahge-sceap* to find the moments revealing the gentler Beowulf. Why then are these the aspects of his character that receive such emphasis in the final evaluation of him? The answer would seem to be that these are the virtues most prominently shared by both pagan and Christian cultures.[54] No Christian in the poet's audience need hesitate to honor Beowulf's memory for such excellent qualities as these. More important, these virtues of Beowulf's are praised not by the poet in his own voice but rather by Beowulf's own people. ("*They* said that he was of the kings of the world the kindest.") The poet reassuringly tells his audience that some at least of the virtues which they had learned to value in their secure Christian milieu had been valued by the men of old as well.

But the *Beowulf* poet apposes one final superlative to make the last word of his poem: Beowulf was *lofgeornost*, "the most eager for praise" or "most vainglorious." Far from the name of a Christian virtue, this word occurs most often in Anglo-Saxon homiletic discussions of the cardinal sins.[55] Bosworth-Toller, it is true, tries to set up a positive sense for the word ("most eager to deserve praise"), but the only documentation for this meaning is the last line in *Beowulf.* Even if there were a positive, Christian sense of *lofgeorn*, would a contemporary of the poet's have thought such a meaning available to the hero's pagan mourners? The audience is by this time far too well-practiced in discriminating between pagan and Christian senses of words, far too aware of how the language of the poem bears witness to the theological predicament of the people described by that language. In *lofgeornost* they could only have seen that the hero lived

81

and died in ignorance of Christian truth. He was gentle, kind, and self-sacrificing and had almost every other virtue. By any human standard of judgment he would seem deserving of a place in Heaven. But human standards are of no consequence in circumstances such as these. It is the judgment of another, more mysterious power that matters here, and none has described that mystery better than Hrothgar in his great speech to Beowulf:

> Wundor is to secganne,
> hu mihtig god   manna cynne
> þurh sidne sefan   snyttru bryttað,
> eard ond eorlscipe.   [1724–27]

"To say how the powerful god, in his vast intelligence, dispenses rewards to men is a subject beyond human understanding."[56] Since no Christian can presume to know with certainty God's judgment of another mortal, a Christian could read a Christian sense into Hrothgar's statement about the mysteriousness of his own god. To read it so, however, profits the souls of Hrothgar and Beowulf but little, although it does give the poet's audience a brief moment of fellowship with those Germanic ancestors, since both stand in the presence of inscrutable powers. But that fellowship can be no lasting union, for the people of Christian England can never reenter the severe, benighted world of the men of old, nor would they. All the poetry of *Beowulf* can do is bring the two together in a brief, loving, and faintly disquieting apposition.

ABBREVIATIONS

BTD Joseph Bosworth, *Anglo-Saxon Dictionary,* ed. and enlarged by T. Northcote Toller (Oxford, 1882–98)
BTS T. Northcote Toller, *An Anglo-Saxon Dictionary: Supplement* (Oxford, 1908–21)
EETS Early English Text Society
ELH *English Literary History*
ELN *English Language Notes*
JEGP *Journal of English and Germanic Philology*
MP *Modern Philology*
PL J.-P. Migne, *Patrologiae cursus completus,* Series secunda (Latina)
RES *Review of English Studies*

NOTES

CHAPTER 1

1. John C. Hodges and Mary E. Whitten, *Harbrace College Handbook*, 8th ed. (New York, 1977), 425.

2. E.g., H. Poutsma, *A Grammar of Late Modern English*, 2d ed. (Groningen, Netherlands, 1928), 278.

3. Fred C. Robinson, "Two Aspects of Variation in Old English Poetry," in *Old English Poetry: Essays on Style*, ed. Daniel G. Calder (Berkeley, 1979), 129.

4. Frederick Klaeber, "Studies in the Textual Interpretation of *Beowulf*," *MP* 3 (1905), 237. Cf. Frederick Klaeber, ed., *Beowulf and the Fight at Finnsburg*, 3d ed. with 1st and 2nd supps. (Boston, 1950), lxv. All quotations from *Beowulf* are drawn from this edition and are cited by simple line number(s). I have not reproduced Klaeber's macrons and other diacritics, and I occasionally disregard his use of capital letters (as is explained in ch. 2, n. 57).

5. *BTD*, s.v. *handgestealla*, brings out well the elemental meaning of the compound with its definition "one whose place is close at one's hand."

6. For this interpretation of "garholt . . . mægenes fultum" (1834–35), see Robinson, "Two Aspects of Variation," 134–35.

7. Some reasons for dissenting from Kenneth Sisam's popular argument that there is no treachery afoot in Heorot (in *The Structure of "Beowulf"* [Oxford, 1965]) are set forth in my essay "Teaching the Backgrounds: History, Religion, and Culture," in *Approaches to Teaching "Beowulf"*, ed. Jess B. Bessinger, Jr., and Robert F. Yeager (New York, 1984), 109, 111–12.

8. Assuming that a finite form of *geþingian* lies behind the MS *geþinged*, I translate "him . . . to hofum Geata / geþinged" as "makes arrangements (or negotiates) for himself at the courts of the Geatas" (*to* being used as in 1990). Although indirectly phrased so as not to alarm Hrothulf, Beowulf's statement makes clear that if the king's son opens negotiations with the Geatas, he will find that he has allies there.

9. J.R.R. Tolkien, "*Beowulf*: The Monsters and the Critics," *Proceedings of the British Academy* 22 (1936), 245–95.

10. Only *El Cid*, the great Spanish epic, is close in time to the events it describes, and its heroic quality is accordingly diminished. The most charming and realistic of medieval epics, *El Cid* is the least heroic in outlook and temper.

11. See Amos's *Linguistic Means of Determining the Dates of Old English Texts* (Cambridge, Mass., 1980); Colin Chase, ed., *The Dating of "Beowulf"* (Toronto, 1981); Kevin S. Kiernan, *"Beowulf" and the "Beowulf" Manuscript* (New Brunswick, 1981).

12. Amos, pp. 100–2.

13. See especially the essays by R.I. Page and Roberta Frank in *The Dating of "Beowulf,"* 113–39.

14. The threefold anathema—"quicumque vult salvus esse: ante omnia opus est, ut teneat catholicam fidem. . . . Quam nisi quisque integram inviolatamque servaverit: absque dubio in æternum peribit. . . . Hæc est fides catholica: quam nisi quisque fideliter firmiterque crediderit, salvus esse non poterit"—was widely known through, inter alia, the liturgy.

15. "He that believeth and is baptised shall be saved; but he that believeth not shall be damned."

16. *Sancti Bonifatii et Lullii epistolae,* ed. M. Tangl, Monumenta historica Germaniae, Epistolae selectae, I (1916), no. 46.

17. *Monumenta Germaniae historica: Epistolae Karolini Aevi,* II (1895), ed. E. Dümmler, 183.

18. For a compilation of Tertullian's uses of this antithesis, see Jean-Claude Fredouille, *Tertullien et la conversion de la culture antique* (Paris, 1972), 320–22.

19. *Epistola* 22, 29, *PL,* XX, col. 416: "Quae enim communicatio luci ad tenebras? Qui consensus Christo cum Belial? Quid facit cum Psalterio Horatius?"

20. *Sancti Bonifatii,* no. 87, and Luc d'Achery, *Spicilegium; sive, Collectio veterum aliquot scriptorum qui in Galliæ bibliothecis delituerant* (Paris, 1723), II, 77.

21. See *Die Hirtenbriefe Ælfrics in altenglischer und lateinischer Fassung,* ed. Bernhard Fehr, reprinted with a supplement to the introduction by Peter Clemoes, Bibliothek der angelsächsischen Prosa 9 (Darmstadt, 1966), 25, and *Wulfstan's Canons of Edgar,* ed. Roger Fowler, EETS, o.s. 266 (London, 1972), 6. For further demonstration that Alcuin's letter accurately represents Christian teaching in Anglo-Saxon England, see now Patrick Wormald, "Bede, *Beowulf,* and the Conversion of the Anglo-Saxon Aristocracy," in *Bede and Anglo-Saxon England: Papers in Honour of the 1300th Anniversary of the Birth of Bede, Given at Cornell University in 1973 and 1974,* ed. Robert T. Farrell, British Archaeological Reports 46 (Oxford, 1978), 43–48.

22. Gale R. Owen's chapter "Pagan Inhumation and Cremation Rites" in her *Rites and Religions of the Anglo-Saxons* (London, 1981), 67–95, provides a summary of pertinent facts. Even generations after the Anglo-Saxons abandoned cremation, they could not have forgotten that it was the way of the heathen, for they continued to encounter it in their contacts with pagan Germanic tribes on the continent: see Boniface's letter to Æthelbald, king of Mercia (*Sancti Bonifatii,* no. 73.) Wormald, p. 40, rightly observes

that cremation never had been "remotely tolerable in Christian circles." See his documentation on p. 75, n. 36.

23. See Owen, pp. 74–75, and Francis Peabody Magoun, Jr., "On Some Survivals of Pagan Beliefs in Anglo-Saxon England," *Harvard Theological Review* 40 (1947), 46, who demonstrates further that the ritually mourning woman and the perambulation of Beowulf's barrow would also have been recognized as distinctively pagan features of the practices in *Beowulf*.

24. Following the passage on Ingeld in his letter to the monks of Lindisfarne, Alcuin vigorously denounces the pagan practice of reading auguries and omens. See also *Sancti Bonifatii*, nos. 50, 51, 56, and 78, and Felix Liebermann, ed., *Die Gesetze der Angelsachsen* (Halle, 1903–13), II, pt. 2, p. 574. Ælfric condemns pagan divination in "De auguriis" in *Ælfric's Lives of Saints*, ed. Walter W. Skeat, 2 vols, EETS, o.s. 76, 82, 94, 114 (London, 1881–1900), I, 364–83 (see p. 370 for explicit prohibition against calculating the best days for travel), and in *Homilies of Ælfric: A Supplementary Collection*, ed. John C. Pope, II, EETS, o.s. 260 (London, 1968), 790–96. The Old English *Distichs of Cato*, no. 30, warn against divining future events by casting lots: see R.S. Cox, "The Old English Dicts of Cato," *Anglia* 90 (1972), 9. Prohibitions against casting of lots were so pervasive that metaphorical uses of terms like *hleotan*, *hlytm*, and *unhlitme* in *Beowulf* may have carried an undertone of pagan associations. See René Derolez, "La divination chez les Germains," in *La divination*, ed. André Caquot and Marcel Leiborici (Paris, 1968), I, 293.

25. Håkan Ringbom, *Studies in the Narrative Technique of "Beowulf" and Lawman's "Brut,"* Acta Academia Aboensis, ser. A Humaniora, XXXVI, no. 2 (Åbo, Finland, 1968), 18, n. 10. For the form *hæðnum*, cf. *Beowulf* 2216.

26. See A.T. Hatto, "Snake-swords and Boar-helms in *Beowulf*," *English Studies* 38 (1957), 145–60, 257–59.

27. We do see the Swedish King Ongentheow threatening to sacrifice warriors to Odin (2939–41), perhaps. See Hilda Ellis Davidson, *Gods and Myths of Northern Europe* (Harmondsworth, England, 1964), 51, and Hans Kuhn, "Gaut," in *Festschrift für Jost Trier zu seinem 60. Geburtstag*, ed. Benno von Weise and Karl Heinz Borck (Meisenheim, West Germany, 1954), 417–33. It seems likely that Ongentheow was alluding more to pagan sacrifices than to some kind of punishment for war crimes.

28. It may have been regarded as impious as well as shocking to name the pagan gods. See Exodus 23:13, Joshua 23:7, Psalms 16:4, Hosea 2:17, and Zachariah 13:2. Tertullian alludes to this scriptural injunction when he says, "The Law prohibits the gods of the nations from being named" (*De idololatria*, ch. 20), and Cynewulf, in his *Juliana*, deletes from his poem the names of pagan gods which are present in his source.

29. *Hæðen* occurs but five times in the entire poem (six if we restore the erased MS reading at 1983). That the word had special force may be suggested by the capital *H* used with the word at *Beowulf* 852 (according to

Thorkelin A), which Kemp Malone finds "particularly striking." See *The Nowell Codex,* Early English Manuscripts in Facsimile, XII, ed. Kemp Malone (Copenhagen, 1963), 20.

30. Larry D. Benson, "The Pagan Coloring of *Beowulf,*" in *Old English Poetry: Fifteen Essays,* ed. Robert P. Creed (Providence, R.I., 1967), 193–213.

31. *Homilies of Ælfric,* ed. Pope, II, 687–88.

32. Cf. the similar concern for Cato's soul in *Purgatorio* I, 73–75.

33. E.G. Stanley, "Hæthenra Hyht in *Beowulf,*" in *Studies in Old English Literature in Honor of Arthur G. Brodeur,* ed. S.B. Greenfield (Eugene, Ore., 1963), 147, points out that the Anglo-Saxon monk of Whitby who wrote the life of Pope Gregory alludes to the Trajan story. See also Charles S. Singleton, trans., *The Divine Comedy: Purgatorio,* II: *Commentary* (Princeton, 1973), 210–13.

34. See G.H. Russell, "The Salvation of the Heathen: The Exploration of a Theme in *Piers Plowman,*" *Journal of the Warburg and Courtauld Institute* 29 (1966), 101–16, and R.W. Chambers, "Long Will, Dante, and the Righteous Heathen," *Essays and Studies by Members of the English Association* 9 (1924), 50–69.

35. See Charles Donahue, "Beowulf, Ireland, and the Natural Good," *Traditio* 7 (1949–51), 263–77, and "Beowulf and Christian Tradition: A Reconsideration from a Celtic Stance," *Traditio* 21 (1965), 55–116.

36. Benson, "The Pagan Coloring," 202–4.

37. Morton Bloomfield, "Patristics and Old English Literature: Notes on Some Poems," in *Studies in Old English Literature in Honor of Arthur G. Brodeur,* ed. Stanley B. Greenfield (Eugene, Ore., 1963), 39–41.

38. The translation is that of Charles S. Singleton, *Purgatorio,* I: *Italian Text and Translation,* 239.

39. Klaeber, *Beowulf and the Fight at Finnsburg,* observes, "Obviously, composition is one of the most striking and inherently significant elements of the diction. . . .Fully one third of the entire vocabulary, or some 1070 words, are compounds, so that in point of numbers, the *Beowulf* stands practically in the front rank of Old English poems" (p. lxiv).

40. See Charles T. Carr, *Nominal Compounds in Germanic,* St. Andrews University Publications 41 (London, 1939), 320–21, 324–43. In Hermann Paul's *Principles of the History of Language,* trans H.A. Strong (London, 1888), various types of compounds are described as "the appositional connexion of two substantives" and "the appositional . . . connexion of two adjectives," etc. (p. 369). A relevant contemporary definition is that of Baxter Hathaway, *A Transformational Syntax* (New York, 1967): "Compound—A construction . . . in which words are juxtaposed without inflectional, derivational, or analytic signals of relationship" (p. 288).

41. Thomas J. Gardner, *Semantic Patterns in Old English Substantival Compounds* (Hamburg, 1968); Carr, *Nominal Compounds in Germanic,* 319–43.

42. Or possibly Hygd: see Norman E. Eliason, "The 'Thryth-Offa Digression' in *Beowulf*," in *Franciplegius: Medieval and Linguistic Studies in Honor of Francis Peabody Magoun, Jr.*, ed. Jess B. Bessinger, Jr., and Robert P. Creed (New York, 1965), 124–38.

43. See Hans Marchand, *The Categories and Types of Present-Day English Word-Formation*, 2d rev. ed. (Munich, 1969), 31–95; cf. Robert B. Lees, *The Grammar of English Nominalizations* (Bloomington, Ind., 1960), and Laurie Bauer, *The Grammar of Nominal Compounding*, Odense University Studies in Linguistics 4 (Odense, Denmark, 1978).

44. For important cautionary strictures on transformational analysis of Old English compounds, see Gardner, *Semantic Patterns*, 31–33.

45. Bruce Mitchell, "The Dangers of Disguise: Old English Texts in Modern Punctuation," *RES*, n.s. 31 (1980), 385–413.

46. Otto Jespersen, *Philosophy of Grammar* (London, 1924), 310.

47. I omit Klaeber's comma after *leod*, which obscures the parallel sentence construction.

48. See "fleogan flana scuras" in *Judith* 221, "fleogende flane" in *Charms* 4:11, "flanes flyht" in *Maldon* 71, "flacor flangeweorc" in *Christ* 676, and "flacor flanþracu" in *Guthlac* 1144. All quotations from poems other than *Beowulf* refer to *The Anglo-Saxon Poetic Records*, ed. George Philip Krapp and Elliott van Kirk Dobbie (New York, 1931–53), 6 vols.

49. Alistair Campbell, "The Use in *Beowulf* of Earlier Heroic Verse," in *England before the Conquest: Studies in Primary Sources presented to Dorothy Whitelock*, ed. Peter Clemoes and Kathleen Hughes (Cambridge, 1971), observes that "the *Beowulf* poet stands practically alone in using the Homeric-Virgilian device of an inserted narrative in its original structural function" of illuminating "the character and background of their heroes" (pp. 283–84). Campbell's examples are different from mine.

50. *Pruðr*, the Old Icelandic equivalent of *þryð*, is the name of a pagan deity. If there were a corresponding figure in the pre-Christian English pantheon, this could have added to the ominous connotations of the name. A further connection with German *Drude*, "witch, evil demon," has been proposed but is etymologically problematic. As Eliason has shown (see n. 42), the status of *Pryð* is questionable. If the name is taken as Modþryð, its significance is no less negative: see *BTD*, s.v. *modþryðu* and *higeþryð*. On Hygd's name, see R. E. Kaske, " 'Hygelac' and 'Hygd,' " in *Studies in Honor of Arthur G. Brodeur*, ed. S. B. Greenfield, reprinted with new "Author's Note" (New York, 1973), 200–6.

51. For the literary uses of names in *Beowulf* and in Old English in general, see Fred C. Robinson, "The Significance of Names in Old English Literature," *Anglia* 86 (1968), 14–58, and "Some Uses of Name-Meanings in Old English Poetry," *Neuphilologische Mitteilungen* 69 (1968), 161–71.

52. Robert E. Kaske, "The Sigemund-Heremod and Hama-Hygelac Passages in *Beowulf*," *PMLA* 74 (1959), 489–94.

53. J.D.A. Ogilvy, "Unferth: Foil to Beowulf?" *PMLA* 79 (1964), 370–75.

54. Contrasts and comparisons between characters in the poem have been skillfully analyzed by Adrien Bonjour, *The Digressions in "Beowulf"*, Medium Ævum Monographs 5 (Oxford, 1950).

55. Fred C. Robinson, "An Introduction to *Beowulf*," in *"Beowulf": A Verse Translation with Treasures of the Ancient North* by Marijane Osborn (Berkeley, 1983), xiv–xv.

56. William Whallon, *Formula, Character, and Context: Studies in Homeric, Old English, and Old Testament Poetry* (Cambridge, Mass., 1969), 98–101, lists nominal formulas for warriors and kings in *Beowulf* and indicates the characters to whom they are applied.

57. Alistair Campbell, "The Use . . . of Earlier Heroic Verse," 283–92, attempts to identify those portions of *Beowulf* which are drawn from preexisting heroic poems.

58. Bonjour, *The Digressions*, 57–61, summarizes the parallels and emphases to which I allude here. For more recent comment, see Donald K. Fry, ed., *Finnsburg: Fragment and Episode* (London, 1974).

59. Late in the preparation of these lectures for the press, I came upon Roberta Frank's splendid essay "The *Beowulf* Poet's Sense of History," in *The Wisdom of Poetry: Essays in Early English Literature in Honor of Morton W. Bloomfield*, ed. Larry Benson and Siegfried Wenzel (Kalamazoo, 1982), 53–65, which treats these phrases as well as other aspects of the *Beowulf* poet's perspective on the heathen past. I have eliminated the discussion of a number of points developed in my original lecture because Frank has dealt with them more skillfully than I did. For a list of the poet's allusions to the fact that his plot takes place in an earlier age, see Klaeber, *Beowulf and the Fight at Finnsburg*, cxxiii, n. 4.

60. "Heard" is the usual rendering, but it is actually imprecise. *Gefrunon* means "asked and received answers," or "learned by asking," the prefix *ge-* imparting perfective sense to the verb *frignan*, "ask." Implicit in *gefrunon*, then, is a confessed eagerness to hear the deeds from olden days, an active interest in the story, and thus *gefrunon* is a bolder word than, say *gehyrdon* when considered in the context of ecclesiastical condemnation of those who listen to songs about the pagan heroes of *geardagum*. This hint at persistent curiosity about the old heroes is carried on in the recurring "ic gefrægn" formula, which contrasts with "ic gehyrde," a verb denoting passive hearing. In other contexts, too, *gefrignan* should be accorded its full semantic force. It is noteworthy, e.g., that Beowulf *gefrægn* rather than *hyrde* the challenge posed by Grendel (194).

CHAPTER 2

1. Frederick Klaeber, "Die christlichen Elemente im *Beowulf*," *Anglia* 35 (1911–12), 134–35.

2. J.R.R. Tolkien, *"Beowulf: The Monsters and the Critics,"* 280–87.

3. Arthur Gilchrist Brodeur, *The Art of "Beowulf"* (Berkeley, 1959), 182–219.

4. I make no effort to survey all attempted explanations of the pagan-Christian question in the poem. A useful conspectus of all but most recent views is Leena Poduschkin's unpublished thesis, "The Religious Elements in *Beowulf*: A Critical Review of Published Opinion" (Helsinki, 1970).

5. Gwyn Jones, *A History of the Vikings* (London, 1973), 73–74, gives the key dates in the conversion of the Northern lands as 965 (Denmark), 1000 (Norway), and 1035 (Sweden). "But for a long while before these definitive changes took place," he emphasizes, "Scandinavia had been isolated in her heathendom." Of course individual Christians must have appeared here and there well before the official dates of the conversions, but no Christians in significant numbers were there as early as the sixth century.

6. Charles Plummer, in his glossary to *Two of the Saxon Chronicles Parallel*, I (Oxford, 1892), 355, s.v. *hæþen*, says, "heathen; in the Chron[icle] practically equivalent to Dane, Danish." *Cartularium Saxonicum*, ed. Walter de Gray Birch, 3 vols. (London, 1885–93), II, nos. 658, 659, 815, etc., specify Danelaw areas as *pagani*. Ælfric's "Passion of St. Edmund, King and Martyr," passim, refers to Danes as "þa hæþenan"; see *Ælfric's Lives of Saints*, ed. Skeat, II, 314–35. See *Maldon* 55, 181; *Capture of the Five Boroughs* 10.

7. But even in the earlier period, Englishmen would have been keenly aware of the paganism of Northern Europe because of the eighth-century Anglo-Saxon missionary work in Germany and Frisia.

8. For the detached, impersonal style of narration, see Peter Clemoes, "Action in *Beowulf* and Our Perception of It," in *Old English Poetry: Essays in Style*, ed. D.G. Calder (Berkeley and Los Angeles, 1979), 147–68. For the relationship between the poet's perspective and style, see E.G. Stanley's precise epigrammatic summation: "An associative imagination works well in annexive syntax: each is the cause of the other's excellence" (*"Beowulf": Continuations and Beginnings*, ed. E.G. Stanley [London, 1966], 136.

9. By "Cædmonian renovation" I mean that process of Christianizing traditional formulas which was supposedly initiated by Cædmon and was carried to completion by the Christian *scopas* who, as Bede's account tells us, followed in his footsteps.

10. The only time anyone but the poet appears to refer to *helle* is in 588, but, as I have pointed out elsewhere, there is no manuscript authority for this occurrence of the word, and the evidence of the Thorkelin transcripts is doubtful. See Fred C. Robinson, "Elements of the Marvelous in the Characterization of *Beowulf*," in *Old English Studies in Honour of John C. Pope*, ed. Robert B. Burlin and Edward B. Irving (Toronto, 1974), 129–30. The poet is also the only one to call Grendel a *deofol*, although Beowulf does say that Grendel's *glof* is made with "deofles cræftum." Possibly the attributive genitive had a generalized sense of "demonic." We should remember too that *deofol* was in the language long before the Christianization of England. It was a Continental loan word introduced directly from Greek. See Karl

Luick, *Historische Grammatik der englischen Sprache,* I (Stuttgart, 1914), 63, 192.

11. Johannes Hoops, *Beowulfstudien* (Heidelberg, 1932), 17–20.

12. *Angelsächsische Homilien und Heiligenleben,* ed. Bruno Assmann, Bibliothek der angelsächsischen Prosa, III (Cassel, West Germany, 1889), 175.

13. *King Alfred's Old English Version of Boethius,* ed. Walter John Sedgefield (Oxford, 1899), 98–99.

14. See *BTD* and *BTS,* s.v. *ent,* for representative examples.

15. Ruth Mellinkoff, "Cain's Monstrous Progeny in *Beowulf,*" *Anglo-Saxon England* 8 (1979), 143–62, and 9 (1980), 183–97, importantly supplements O.F. Emerson's early study, "Legends of Cain, Especially in Old and Middle English," *PMLA* 21 (1906), 831–929. See also my "Lexicography and Literary Criticism: A Caveat," in *Philological Essays: Studies in Old and Middle English Language and Literature in Honour of Herbert Dean Meritt,* ed. James L. Rosier (The Hague, 1970), 102–4.

16. For a thorough exploration of the dual significance of dragons in the Middle Ages, see Jacques le Goff, "Culture ecclésiastique et culture folklorique au Moyen Age: Saint Marcel de Paris et la dragon," in *Pour un autre Moyen Age: Temps, travail, et culture en Occident* (Paris, 1977), 286–79. For a recent careful examination of the dragon in *Beowulf* and its background and meaning, see Alan K. Brown, "The Firedrake in *Beowulf,*" *Neophilologus* 64 (1980), 439–60.

17. The poet uses a similar characterizing device in 2029–69, where Beowulf assesses the prospects of the Ingeld-Freawaru match as poor. Since the audience knows that years later events turned out much as Beowulf predicted, this speech establishes the hero's acumen as a reader of royal politics and of human nature.

18. Johannes Hoops, *Kommentar zum Beowulf* (Heidelberg, 1932), makes this assumption and remarks on the incongruity of a pagan Dane singing a Christian creation hymn: "Den Dänen, die nach 180ff. noch als Heiden gedacht sind, trägt der Sänger hier in einem epischen Lied auffallenderweise die biblische Schöpfungsgeschichte vor, wie se Ælmihtiga zeigt. . . . Sonst kommen am dänischen Hof nur volkstümliche Stoffe aus der german[ischen] Sagengeschichte zum Vortrag: 865–915 Sigemund und Heremod, 1066–1159 der Kampf um Finnsburg" (p. 27). Of course there have been several references to God earlier in the poem (13, 16, 17, 72, etc.), but these are all spoken by the poet in his own voice and therefore have nothing to do with the question of the religious status of the characters in the poem.

19. It is reasonable (but by no means necessary) in part because the poet's terms for a higher being in indirect discourse tend to agree with the terms used in direct discourse by the characters whose speech he is reporting. Hrothgar is the only character in the poem to refer to God with the noun *alwealda* (928, 955), and when the poet reports Hrothgar's waiting to see whether God would ever bring remedy to his woes (1314), he uses the term *alwalda* [MS *alfwalda*]. Hrothgar is also the only character to use the epithet

mihtig of God (1716, 1725), and when the poet reports Hrothgar's thanking God in 1398, he uses the term "mihtigan drihtne." Beowulf uses "ece drihten" and *waldend* in direct discourse (2796, 1661), and the poet uses these terms also when he is reporting Beowulf's speech (2329, 2330), but he is not the only character to use these terms.

20. Richard Cleasby and Gudbrand Vigfusson, *An Icelandic-English Dictionary* with a supplement by Sir William A. Craigie (Oxford, 1957), s.v. *al-máttigr*. This oath, says Cleasby, "implies its use in very early times." Assumptions about Germanic pagan vocabulary based on Old Icelandic material are of course problematic, especially in light of Walter Baetke's "Christlicher Lehngut in der Sagareligion," *Berichte über die Verhandlungen der Sächsischen Akademie der Wissenschaften zu Leipzig*, Philologische-historische Klasse, XCVIII (1951), fasc. 6, 7–55, reprinted in *Kleine Schriften* (Weimar, 1973), 319–50. (I am indebted to Theodore Andersson for locating this reference.) But the Old English terminology for God and Christian practices *is* by and large Germanic, not foreign, in origin and must at one time have referred to religious practices other than Christian. If, moreover, the reciprocal influence between terminologies took place in Old English, as Baetke assumes, it would seem to confirm the ambiguity of these words.

21. We have it on the authority of *Hrólfs saga Kraka* that one of the Danes in Heorot, Hrothulf (Hrólfr), was a pagan who never sacrificed to the gods. See Gerd Wolfgang Weber, "Irreligiosität und Heldenzeitalter: Zum Mythencharakter der altisländischen Literatur," in *Speculum Norroenum: Norse Studies in Memory of Gabriel Turville-Petre*, ed. Ursula Dronke et al. (Odense, Denmark, 1981), 474–505. For the phrase "the all-powerful being (whoever he might be)," see Lönnroth, "The Noble Heathen," cited in n. 25 below.

22. The same is true of the semantically equivalent compound *Alvaldr* (OE *alwalda*), which, in secular contexts, means "sovereign king" or "the powerful."

23. Christine Fell, "Hild, Abbess of Streonæshalch," in *Hagiography and Medieval Literature: A Symposium*, ed. Hans Bekker-Nielsen et al. (Odense, Denmark, 1981), 97.

24. On the adaptation of Old English poetic vocabulary to Christian uses, see Albert Keiser, *The Influence of Christianity on the Vocabulary of Old English Poetry*, University of Illinois Studies in Language and Literature, V nos. 1 and 2 (Urbana, 1919). Cf. Helmut Gneuss, *Lehnbildungen und Lehnbedeutungen im Altenglischen* (Berlin, 1955). On the "Polysemie infolge von Bedeutungsentlehnung," see Herbert Koziol, *Grundzüge der englischen Semantik*, Wiener Beiträge zur englischen Philologie 70 (1967), 31–35.

25. See Lars Lönnroth, "The Noble Heathen: A Theme in the Sagas," *Scandinavian Studies* 41 (1969), 1–29, along with the important qualification in his "Iǫrð fannz œva ne upphiminn: A Formula Analysis," in *Specu-*

lum Norroenum, ed. Dronke et al., 326, n. 26. Lönnroth's idea is partially anticipated by Francis B. Gummere, *Founders of England,* with supplementary notes by Francis Peabody Magoun (New York, 1930), 340–41.

26. Lönnroth, "The Noble Heathen," 1, 13.

27. *The Old English Orosius,* ed. Janet Bately, EETS, S.S. 6 (London, 1980), p. 59, 11. 23–27.

28. Ibid., p. 103, 11. 27–29.

29. E.g., in the metrum "Si uis celsi iura tonantis" (IV.vi), which in the Old English begins, "Gif ðu nu wilnige weorulddrihtnes / heane anwald hlutre mode / ongitan giorne, gem almægene / heofones tunglu." See Sedgefield, p. 200.

30. *Aeneid* I, 603–5: "Di tibi, si qua pios respectant numina, si quid / usquam iustitia est et mens sibi conscia recti, / praemia digna ferant." The temple to the unknown god in Book VIII would also be relevant here.

31. The idea that pagans might perceive the Creator through his creation is in accord with St. Paul's explanation of how the Gentiles could gain an understanding of God without Christian evangelists (Romans 1:20) and was a common theme in the "noble heathen" motif in the sagas. See Lönnroth, "The Noble Heathen," passim.

32. The Old English *Boethius* reminds us that Homer "oft ond gelome / þære sunnan wlite swiðe herede, / æðelo cræftas . . . / leoðum," etc. (Sedgefield, p. 203), and in *Aeneid* I, 742–43, the minstrel Iopas sings of the creation of man and animals and sun and moon in terms similar to those of the scop in *Beowulf.* The fourth stanza of *Vǫluspá* takes up the same subject. Lars Lönnroth, "Iǫrð fannz œva ne upphiminn," has shown how oral formulas and themes relating to creation songs served poets equally in pre-Christian and Christian times, so that the same phrases occur in Old English, Old Saxon, Old High German, and Old Norse poems, sometimes with Christian reference, sometimes with pagan. Cf. also G. Schütte, "Die Schöpfungssagen in Deutschland und im Norden," *Indogermanische Forschungen* 17 (1905), 444–57.

33. Whallon, *Formula, Character and Context,* 119–22, displays, by reference to Old Norse, the probable pagan meanings of the terms for "god" in *Beowulf.* I cite his findings gratefully while at the same time disagreeing with his conclusion that *Beowulf* "is not Christian in any important manner at all" (p. 132).

34. The ambiguity of such words in Old English is illustrated by Wulfstan's chapter headings, such as "Be heofonlicum cyninge" and "Be eorðlicum cyninge" at the beginning of the *Institutes of Polity,* and by Alcuin's famous antithesis of "rex caelestis" and "the so-called kings, who are heathen and damned" in his letter to the monks of Lindisfarne. See above, ch. 1, n. 17.

35. *The Death of Edgar* has "freolic wealdend" (l. 6) and "hæleða wealdend" (l. 8), while *The Coronation of Edgar* has "Engla waldend" (l. 1).

36. See *BTD,* s.v. *wealdend.*

37. *The Old English Orosius*, ed. Bately, p. 25, 11. 11–13.

38. Ibid., p. 139.

39. Joseph Bosworth, *King Alfred's Anglo-Saxon Version of the Compendious History of the World by Orosius* (London, 1859), 120.

40. Quoted in *The Old English Orosius*, ed. Bately, 325.

41. The same is true in modern vernaculars which do not use definite and indefinite articles. In modern Finnish, for example, the sentence "häntä on auttanut jumala" would mean "he was helped by a god" if it occurred in a translation of Homer describing Apollo assisting Hector in battle; but in a Christian context the same sentence would mean "he was helped by God." In written Finnish the ambiguity is removed by capitalizing the first letter of *Jumala* when the word refers to God, but in spoken Finnish the sentence is perfectly ambiguous.

42. Sedgefield, p. 247.

43. Ephraim Emerton, in his introduction to *The Letters of St. Boniface* (1940; reprint, New York, 1976), 4.

44. Ursula and Peter Dronke, "The Prologue of the *Prose Edda*: Explorations of a Latin Background," *Sjötíu ritgerðir helgaðar Jakobi Benediktssyni* (Reykjavík, Iceland, 1977), I, 160, 166–67.

45. Hertha Marquardt, *Die altenglischen Kenningar* (Halle, 1938), 287, counts 88 occurrences of *engla* collocations in terms for God.

46. Marquardt, pp. 291–92, reveals how common these terms are in other poetry.

47. Keiser, *The Influence of Christianity*, 72; cf. p. 76.

48. It may be useful to list the terms for a higher being used by the characters in the poem and by the poet. Beowulf refers to a higher being directly 13 times: *dryhten* (441, 686, 2796), *frea* (2794), *god* (570, 685, 1658, 2469), *metod* (967, 979, 2527), *waldend* (1661), and *wuldurcyning* (2795); and 4 times in indirect discourse: *anwalda* (1272), *dryhten* (2330), *god* (227), and *waldend* (2329). Hrothgar refers to a higher being directly 15 times: *alwealda* (928, 955), *dryhten* (940, 1779, 1841), *god* (381, 478, 930, 1716, 1725, 1751), *hyrde* (931), *metod* (945, 1778), *waldend* (1752); and 3 times in indirect discourse: *alwalda* (1314), *dryhten* (2330), and *god* (625). Hygelac once uses the word *god* (1997). The scop uses *ælmihtig* only in indirect discourse (92). The shore guard uses *fæder alwalda* directly once (316). Wiglaf uses *god* twice (2650, 2874), and *waldend* twice (2875, 3109). Wealhtheow uses *god* once in indirect discourse (625). Geatas use *god* twice in indirect discourse (227, 1626). The poet's terms (in addition to those already cited as indirect discourse by characters) include *agend* (3075), *demend* (181), *dryhten* (108, 181, 187, 696, 1554, 1692), *fæder* (188, 1609), *frea* (27), *god* (13, 72, 113, 181, 701, 711, 786, 811, 1056, 1271, 1553, 1682, 2182, 2858, 3054), *helm* (182), *kyningwuldor* (665), *metod* (110, 169, 180, 670, 706, 1057, 1611), *liffrea* (16), *rædend* (1555), *scyppend* (106), *soðcyning* (3055), *waldend* (17, 183, 1693, 2292, 2857).

49. On *sum* meaning "notable, important," see C.L. Wrenn's edition, *"Beowulf" with the Finnesburg Fragment,* rev. and enlarged ed. (London, 1958), 290, and Fred C. Robinson, "The American Element in *Beowulf,*" *English Studies* 49 (1968), 508–16.

50. See, e.g., "soð cyning" in *Juliana* 224; "soð metod" in *Genesis* 1414, 2793, *Exodus* 479, *Andreas* 1601, *Prayer* 27, etc.; "soð sunu metodes" in *Daniel* 401, *Elene* 461, 564, etc.; "soð god" in *Phoenix* 622, *Paris Psalter* 70:11,2, 87:14,2. Elsewhere in the poetry occur terms for God such as "soð sigora frea," "soð fæder," "soð dryhten," "soð sigedrihten," "soð sigora waldend," "soð sunu wealdendes." *Ælfric's Lives of Saints,* ed. Skeat, I, 98, illustrates the significance of "soð god" neatly: "Ge [pagans] habbað manega godas and manega gydena / we soðlice wurðian ænne soðne god." The convert Claudius says, "Ic oncneow to soþan / þæt þin god is soð god and ic sylf nu bidde / þæt þu me geþingie hu ic wurðe his biggenga" (ibid., II, 388). See further Keiser, *The Influence of Christianity,* 71–72.

51. *Homilies of Ælfric,* ed. Pope, II, 677, 681; *Homilies of Wulfstan,* ed. Dorothy Bethurum (Oxford, 1957), 222 et passim.

52. *The Old English Orosius,* ed. Bately, p. 24, 11. 9–13.

53. Ibid., p. 57, 1. 9.

54. *The Old English Version of Bede's Ecclesiastical History of the English People,* ed. Thomas Miller, EETS, o.s. 95 (London, 1890), 136–38.

55. *Venerabilis Bædae Historia ecclesiastica gentis Anglorum,* ed. Charles Plummer (Oxford, 1896), I, 65.

56. E.g., *Meters of Boethius* 19, 36 ("selfa god"), 29, 75 ("self cyning"), 7, 37 ("drihten selfa"), *Elene* 488 ("seolfne Crist"), *Genesis* 1797 ("sigora selfcyning" [or, as some editors prefer, "sigora self cyning"]), *Genesis* 139 ("þeoden self"), 1112, 1270 ("selfa sigora waldend"), 1390 ("selfa drihten"), *Psalm 50* 102, 108 ("god selfa").

57. *Vercelli Homilies IX–XXIII,* ed. Paul E. Szarmach (Toronto, 1981), 23. Here and elsewhere I have henceforth restored the scribes' uncapitalized initial letters in nomina sacra.

58. *Ælfric's Lives of Saints,* ed. Skeat, II, 388, 11. 185–87.

59. *The Prose Edda by Snorri Sturluson,* trans. Arthur Gilchrist Brodeur (New York, 1916), 5.

60. E.g., *Elene* 170, 367; *Daniel* 12, 26, 456 (see especially 577–79, 624–26, and cf. 650–51); *Juliana* 212–24.

61. E.g., "we comon hider . . . þæt ge eowere deofolgild forlæton and oncnawan þone soðan god þe on heofonum is" (*Ælfric's Catholic Homilies, the Second Series: Text,* ed. Malcolm Godden, EETS, s.s. 5 [London, 1979], 280); "ac gehyrað nu þone soþan god eowerne scyppend þe on heofenum eardað and ne gelyfe ge heononforð on ydelum anlicnyssum" (*The Homilies of the Anglo-Saxon Church: The First Part, Containing the Sermones Catholici . . . ,* ed. Benjamin Thorpe, I [London, 1844], 464); "ðe gedafenode . . . þæt ðu oncneuwe þinne deman þe on heofenum is and hine wurðodest se þe

is soð god: and þin mod awendest fram þam leasum godum" (ibid., 588); "nis na godes wunung on ðam grægum stanum ne on ærenum wecgum ac he wunað on heofonum" *Ælfric's Lives of Saints,* ed. Skeat, I, 178); "ic me gebidde to ðam gode þe bið eardigende on heofonum . . . Wod bið se ðe bit æt blindum stanum" (ibid., p. 144).

62. *Homilies of Ælfric,* ed. Pope, II, 710–11, 635–36.

63. Hoops, *Kommentar,* 90, calls it "ein verblasster Ausdruck aus der Terminologie des altgermanischen Schicksalsglaubens," while Klaeber, *"Beowulf" and the Fight at Finnsburg,* insists (p. 154) that it is "a mere figure of speech." But "gewif, gewef" glosses both *textura* and "fortuna, fata" in Anglo-Saxon manuscripts, and the weaving of one's *wyrd* is alluded to explicitly in *Riming Poem* 70 and *Guthlac* 1351 (cf. *Riddle* 35, 9). We may wonder, moreover, whether figures of speech are "mere" when they occur in poetry.

64. *Dryhten* was one of the terms given new Christian meaning by the Cædmonian renovation of Old English poetic diction. Old Norse *dróttinn* seems to have been "used of supernatural beings in general" (Thor, Freyr, giants, demons) in pre-Christian usage. Wulfila declined to use the Gothic cognate as a term for the Christian God, either because he disliked the implications of comitatus reciprocity between lord and follower or, as de Vries and others have thought, because it was too closely associated with pagan gods. See D.H. Green, *The Carolingian Lord: Semantic Studies in Four Old High German Words: Balder, Frô, Truhtin, Hêrro* (Cambridge, 1965), 529, 266–68; cf. 534–35.

65. "Kveld lifir maðr ekki / eptir kvið norna." See *The Poetic Edda,* I: *Heroic Poems,* ed. Ursula Dronke (Oxford, 1969), 167. Cf. Gunnar's remark, "Death will catch up with me wherever I am, when it is so fated" *(Njal's Saga,* trans. Magnus Magnusson and Hermann Pálsson [Harmondsworth, England, 1960], 156).

66. The original meaning of *metod* was "measure": see Julius Pokorny, *Indogermanisches etymologisches Wörterbuch* (Bern, 1954), pp. 705–6: *metod* is "what is measured out (i.e., fate)" or "the measurer (of men's spans)." Old Icelandic *mjǫtuðr* refers to pagan deities, to fate, and to death. In *Waldere* 1, 19 *metod* seems to mean "fate" or "fated death." The feminine form of the word is used by King Alfred to translate Latin *Parcae* in the *Boethius:* "metena [*v.l.* gydena], ðe folcisce men hatað Parcae" (Sedgefield, p. 102).

67. Brodeur, *The Art of "Beowulf,"* 193, also thinks *metod* here refers to fate, not God.

68. In a quite different context, Thomas D. Hill has recently demonstrated that *metod* in Old English poetry carried both its primitive sense "measurer" and its Christian sense "God" and that poets played on the two meanings. See "The Measure of Hell: *Christ and Satan* 695–722," *Philological Quarterly* 60 (1981), 409–14.

69. *Aldhelmi opera omnia,* ed. Rudolf Ehwald, Monumenta Germaniae

historica, auctorum antiqissimorum XV (Berlin, 1919), 126. Cf. p. 321, 11. 4–11, where, in the *De virginitate*, a flowery invocation of the Fates is yoked with the soberer phrase "with Christ's cooperation."

70. Birch, *Cartularium Saxonicum*, II, nos. 595, 941, 960, 1196. Since *tonans* and *sator* are Classical Latin terms for Jupiter, these references to "the high thunderer" and "the supreme thunderer" must have had some pagan Classical overtones.

71. Cf. Christine Mohrmann, "La langue et le style de la poésie latine chrétienne," *Etudes sur le Latin des Chrétiens*, I (Rome, 1961), 151–68.

72. See Gernot Wieland, *The Latin Glosses on Arator and Prudentius in Cambridge University Library MS. Gg.5.35*, Pontifical Institute of Mediaeval Studies, Studies and Texts 61 (Toronto, 1983), 36–37 and glossary, s.v. *numen* and *tonans*; cf. *deus, olympas, omnipotens*, and *regnator*.

73. On cento, see F.J.E. Raby, *A History of Christian-Latin Poetry from the Beginning to the Close of the Middle Ages*, 2d ed. (Oxford, 1953), 16; Octave Delepierre, *Tableau de la littérature du centon, chez les anciens et chez les modernes*, 2 vols. (London, 1874–75); and Rose Lamacchia, "Dall' arte allusiva al centone," *Atene e Roma*, n.s. 3 (1958), 193–216.

74. For a valuable discussion of the pagan and Christian meanings of *metod, wyrd, bealdor*, and other words as these have been understood by philologists at different times during the past 150 years, see E.G. Stanley, *The Search for Anglo-Saxon Paganism* (Cambridge, 1975). Although Stanley's primary concern is to expose the excesses of the early practitioners of *Deutschtümelei*, his analyses reveal the semantic complexity of the words discussed. His summation of the semantic properties of *wyrd* in *Solomon and Saturn*, e.g., states precisely what I take to be the situation in *Beowulf*: "To the heathen, who see only immediate effects and know nothing of their ultimate cause, *wyrd* seems baleful, a subject for gloomiest speculation and darkest fear; Christians, and among them the Old English poets, recognize in *wyrd* the executive aspect of an ultimately beneficent divine power" (p. 121).

75. See Green, *The Carolingian Lord*, 289–91, and Green's later article "Old English *Dryht*: A New Suggestion," *Modern Language Review* 63 (1968), 398. For Pope Gregory's letter, see *Historia ecclesiastica*, ed. Plummer, I, 64–66. Pope Gregory had second thoughts on his advice to Mellitus and advised King Ethelbert to destroy pagan shrines; cf. p. 68. And yet the conceit of rededicating pagan temples to Christian use rather than destroying them retained its appeal: see *Ælfric's Lives of Saints*, ed. Skeat, II, p. 250, 11. 479–83.

76. *Die Hirtenbriefe Ælfrics*, ed. Fehr, p. 126, 1. 26.

77. *The Old English Orosius*, ed. Bately, p. 66, 1. 29.

78. *Vǫluspá*, ed. Sigurður Nordal, trans. B.S. Benedikz and John McKinnell, Durham and St. Andrews Texts 1 (Durham, England, 1978), 116, and *The Prose Edda by Snorri Sturluson*, trans. Brodeur, 31.

79. Graham D. Caie discusses the word at length in *The Judgment Day Theme in Old English Poetry* (Copenhagen, 1976).

80. The Germanic conception of the gods as disposers of men's lives and determiners of their destinies is reflected not only in *metod* (OIcel. *mjǫtuðr*) but also, perhaps, in OIcel. *regin*, "the powers who decide" (cf. Gothic *ragin*, "decision").

81. F.P. Magoun, "On Some Survivals of Pagan Belief," 33–42, suggests that *mægen* in *Beowulf* referred originally to pagan Germanic mana but has been "colored" by the Christian poet with the notion of Heavenly Grace (p. 42).

82. See Mechthild Gretsch, *Die Regula Sancti Benedicti in England und ihre altenglische Übersetzung,* Texte und Untersuchungen zur englischen Philologie 2 (Munich, 1973), pp. 347–49.

83. Frank, "The *Beowulf* Poet's Sense of History," 54.

84. The tone is one of regret, not condescension. Cf. *Aeneid* XII, 899–900: "Vix illud lecti bis sex cervice subirent, / qualia nunc hominum producit corpora tellus." The men of old were not like us.

85. On terms for grace, see Marie Padgett Hamilton, "The Religious Principle in *Beowulf,*" *PMLA* 61 (1946), 312–13, n. 21, and Klaus Faiss, *"Gnade" bei Cynewulf und seiner Schule,* Studien zur englischen Philologie, n.s. 12 (Tubingen, 1967).

86. Since dictionaries enter "virtue" as a meaning of *cræft,* a sceptic might object that the components of *mægencræft* are not semantically contrastive after all. But the use of *cræft* to render Christian *virtus* is an idiosyncrasy of King Alfred and not, apparently, normal Old English. See Gretsch p. 348. Thomas Gardner has argued persuasively that even when the two elements of *mægencræft* (and similar compounds) are assumed to be synonymous, the first element probably has an intensifying function, so that *mægencræft,* "mægenes cræft," etc., are not merely tautological in any case. See Gardner, *Semantic Patterns,* 72–73, 111–13.

87. The pre-Christian and Christian senses of *synn* and *firen* are defined in Gneuss, *Lehnbildungen,* 87.

88. In his glossary Klaeber gives "crime, sin, wicked deed" as the only meanings of *firen,* but see his discussion of *firen* and *synn* in "Die christlichen Elemente im *Beowulf,*" 128, n. 1.

89. See Joseph Weisweiler, "Beiträge zur Bedeutungsentwicklung germanischer Wörter für sittliche Begriffe," *Indogermanische Forschungen* 41 (1929), 70–77, who says the original meaning of Germanic **balwa-* was "tückisches Angreifen" or *Quälerei.* (The basic meaning of the Indo-European root **bheleu-,* according to Pokorny, *Indogermanisches etymologisches Wörterbuch,* 125, was "schlagen, durch Schlagen kraftlos machen, schwach, krank.") Cf. Friedrich Schubel, "Zur Bedeutungskunde altenglischer Wörter mit christlichem Sinngehalt," *Archiv für das Studium der neueren Sprachen* 189 (1953), 289–303, and "Die Bedeutungsnuancen von *bealu* in *Christ* I–III," in *Festschrift zum 75. Geburtstag von Theodor Spira* (Heidelberg, 1961), 328–34.

90. None of the nouns that stand in apposition with *bealu* compounds is

a word of moral condemnation; all express conflict or violence pure and simple: "feorhbealo . . . guðdeað, "hild . . . feorhbealu," "guð . . . feorhbealu," "gewinnes weorc . . . leodbealu," "leodbealewa . . . inwitniða," "morðbealu . . . fæhðe ond fyrene," "nydwracu . . . nihtbealwe," "fæhð . . . bealonið."

91. *Ælfric's Lives of Saints*, ed. Skeat, II, 220.

92. Blaise Pascal, *Pensées*, preface et intro. by Léon Brunschvicg (Paris, 1972), 219.

93. Christopher Ricks, *Milton's Grand Style* (Oxford, 1963), 109–17.

CHAPTER 3

1. Klaeber, *Beowulf and the Fight at Finnsburg*, lxvi.

2. See, e.g., the apposition "se grimma gæst . . . mære mearcstapa" (102–3), which the poet uses to swing his focus from Grendel's malevolent character to his habitat (which then becomes the subject of the ensuing lines); or "feorh . . . hæþene sawle" (851–52), which moves attention from where Grendel dies to the fate of his soul: "Þær him hel onfeng."

3. Cf. the Blickling Homilist's reference to "doers of good" with the words "godes wyrhtan" in *The Blickling Homilies of the Tenth Century*, EETS, o.s. 58, 63, 73, 1 vol. ed. Richard Morris (London, 1874–80), 111. The common collocation *godes ond yfeles* exemplifies *god* in the same sense.

4. The immediately preceding reference to Beówulf as "secg on searwum . . . wæpnum geweorðad" would probably lead the audience to think first of external ornamentation when it hears *wlite;* but the shoreguard is questioning not whether the hero is worthy of his weapons but rather whether he is as noble as his peerless countenance suggests. Cf. Fred C. Robinson, "Two Non-Cruces in *Beowulf*," *Tennessee Studies in Literature* 11 (1966), 155–60.

5. This apposition is of interest as the only direct evidence in the poem that Breca was not a mere boyhood friend of Beowulf's but a young ruler. This is confirmed in *Widsith* 25: "Breoca [weold] Brondingum."

6. The same metaphor occurs elsewhere. *Goldhord* is used of Christ, e.g., in both prose and poetry: see *The Christ of Cynewulf*, ed. Albert S. Cook (Boston, 1900), 1. 787, and the note to this line on p. 151. *Heahgestreonum* is apparently used to refer to Christ and Andrew in *Andreas* 362. For this and other instances of the metaphor, see Hans Schabram, "*Andreas* und *Beowulf*: Parallelstellen als Zeugnis für literarische Abhängigkeit," *Nachrichten der Giessener Hochschulgesellschaft* 34 (1965), 215–16.

7. For a remarkable instance in which the poet revivifies the worn metaphor of life's banquet and death's sleep, see 1002–20, discussed in ch. 1 above.

8. See R.E. Kaske, "*Sapientia et Fortitudo* as the Controlling Theme of *Beowulf*," *Studies in Philology* 55 (1958), 423–56.

9. Cf. *ænigre* (949), *weorþre* (1902), *sorge* (2004), *yrmðe* (2005), *sigehwile* (2710), etc.

10. And there are more. E.g., "grundwyrgenne . . . merewif mihtig" (1518–19), "dædcene mon . . . hæle hildedeor" (1645–46), "goldwlanc . . . since hremig" (1881–82), "hearpan wynne . . . gomenwudu" (2107–8), "holmwylme . . . yðgewinne" (2411–12), "eorla sum . . . æþele cempa" (1312). This last example shows *æþele* reinforcing emphatic *sum*, "notable, outstanding." See ch. 2, n. 49 on emphatic *sum*.

11. The original sense may have been "person with a membrum virile," but the word could easily have been interpreted popularly as "the sex which bears arms."

12. See Julius Pokorny, *Indogermanisches etymologisches Wörterbuch,* 746–47.

13. *The Harley Latin-Old English Glossary, edited from British Museum Manuscript Harley 3376,* by Robert T. Oliphant (The Hague, 1964), 101.

14. Caroline Brady, " 'Warriors' in *Beowulf:* an Analysis of the Nominal Compounds and an Evaluation of the Poet's Use of Them," *Anglo-Saxon England* 11 (1982), 210–14.

15. See Hatto, "Snake-swords and Boar-helms in *Beowulf,*" 145–60, 257–59, and George Speake, *Anglo-Saxon Animal Art and Its Germanic Background* (Oxford, 1980), 78–81.

16. Klaeber's reconstruction and interpretation of the passage are accepted here, although other interpretations would be consonant with the present account of the boar images.

17. We should remember that, even after the conversion, makers of Anglo-Saxon helmets invoked supernatural powers to defend the wearer. See the crosses and inscriptions on the recently discovered Coppergate helmet (dated by Dominic Tweddle between 750 and 775) and the cross *and* boar image on the Benty Grange helmet.

18. On *frea* (and *bealdor*) as terms for pagan gods, see Green, *The Carolingian Lord,* 50–51, 490.

19. Since *segn* elsewhere in *Beowulf* means "banner" rather than "sign," some readers might prefer translating *Beowulf* 2152b as "a boar banner, a banner of special importance." But it is hard to believe that the meaning "sign" was unknown to the *Beowulf* poet and his audience. *Segn* meaning "sign" is documented elsewhere in Old English poetry (e.g., *Genesis* 2372), and the rather common derivatives *segnian* and *segnung* refer exclusively to the root *segn* in its meaning "sign, numinous image."

20. Gale R. Owen, *Rites and Religions of the Anglo-Saxons,* has observed that "the poet ironically focuses on the boar figure (the protective symbol which decorated a helmet) demonstrating, without needing to expand the point, that the pagan talisman had proved useless" (p. 86).

21. Walther Paetzel, *Die Variationen in der altgermanischen Alliterationspoesie,* 172–73, notes that a larger number of appositions with inanimate referents is found in *Beowulf* than in most Old English poems.

22. Carr, *Nominal Compounds in Germanic,* p. 446.

23. See Genesis 3:17–19. This commonplace is documented in Old English texts, in an eighth-to-ninth-century Einsiedeln manuscript, in Old Icelandic, and elsewhere: see *The Prose "Solomon and Saturn" and "Adrian and Ritheus,"* ed. James E. Cross and Thomas D. Hill (Toronto, 1982), 111–12.

24. *The Old English Orosius,* ed. Bately, 36.

25. *Exameron Anglice,* ed. S.J. Crawford, Bibliothek der angelsächsischen Prosa 10 (Hamburg, 1921), 68–70; *Homilies of Ælfric,* ed. Pope, II, 678–79; cf. Isidore of Seville, *De ordine creaturarum, PL* 83, col. 944.

26. *PL* LXXXIII, col. 825–68.

27. For a fuller treatment of the medieval view of nature, see *Approaches to Nature in the Middle Ages,* ed. Lawrence D. Roberts, Medieval and Renaissance Texts and Studies 16 (Binghamton, 1982), especially the initial essay by Bernard F. Huppé. Earlier scholars who speak of the Anglo-Saxons' "love of [nature's] wilder and more melancholy aspects" and their "early delight in grand and wild aspects" of nature seem to confuse description with admiration. See Stanley, *The Search for Anglo-Saxon Paganism,* 1–3.

28. Dorothy Whitelock, *Anglo-Saxon Wills* (Cambridge, 1930), passim.

29. Dorothy Whitelock, *The Beginnings of English Society* (Harmondsworth, England, 1952), 223.

30. Ibid., 224.

31. George Clark, "Beowulf's Armor," *ELH* 32 (1965), 409–41.

32. The poet sometimes places literal and metaphorical uses of the words in close proximity, as if to ensure that the full force of the metaphor will be felt. Thus *eodor,* "king," in 1044 is used just seven lines after *eodor,* "house" (or "part of a house"); *helm,* "prince," in 1623 is followed by *helm,* "helmet," in 1629.

33. See 801–5, 681–83. Beowulf's renunciation of weapons in fighting Grendel is itself in conformity with the man-made principle of fair play in combat, and his noble gesture turns out to be his salvation and the end of Grendel. But as the melting sword blade suggests, monstrous power itself survives the death of Grendel.

34. *Hring* in the preceding sentence refers explicitly to the protecting rings of the linked battle byrnie. Cf. Hertha Marquardt, "Fürsten- und Kriegerkenning in *Beowulf,*" *Anglia* 60 (1935), 390–95.

35. Edward B. Irving, Jr., *A Reading of "Beowulf"* (New Haven, 1968), 20.

36. Thomas Hobbes, *Leviathan* (London, 1651), 62.

37. See especially Ilse Blumenstengl, *Wesen und Funktion des Banketts im "Beowulf"* (Marburg, 1964).

38. E.A. Thompson, *The Visigoths in the Time of Ulfila* (Oxford, 1966), 68.

39. The text is that of Klaeber, who emends *swa noc* to *swanas.*

Although other editors have emended differently, all seem to agree that the sense is that the retinue repaid the king's mead with loyalty in battle.

40. The text is Dobbie's, except that I have restored MS *gemunu* for reasons spelled out in "Some Aspects of the *Maldon* Poet's Artistry," *JEGP* 75 (1976), 35–37.

41. Snorri Sturluson, *Heimskringla: Sagas of the Norse Kings,* trans. Samuel Laing, rev. Peter Foote (London, 1961), 34.

42. In the poem *Helgakviða Hiǫrvarðssonar,* Hedin, being bewitched, vows *at Bragarfulli* to marry his brother's wife, thereby setting in motion the tragic course of the tale; in the *Jómsvíkinga Saga* (ed. and trans. N.F. Blake [London, 1962], 28–29), Swein Forkbeard, after serving his followers drink and allowing them time to consume it, asks that each make his vow. They do so in orderly sequence.

43. Standing to drink is a custom also alluded to in the *Anglo-Saxon Chronicle* entry for 1042, where Harðacnut "at his drince stod" *(Two of the Saxon Chronicles Parallel,* ed. Plummer, I, 162).

44. "Omnia quæ poti temulento prompsimus ore, / Fortibus edamus animis et vota sequamur / Per summum jurata Jovem superosque potentes."

45. Charles W. Kennedy, trans., *"Beowulf": The Oldest English Epic* (New York, 1940).

46. E. Talbot Donaldson, trans., *"Beowulf": A New Prose Translation* (New York, 1966).

47. John Lesslie Hall, trans., *"Beowulf,"* an Anglo-Saxon Epic Poem (Boston, 1892).

48. Hoops, *Kommentar,* p. 154. Hoops reviews various editors' suggestion that *doð* be emended to imperative singular *do* or that *doð* be read as imperative plural and concludes, rightly, that the imperative makes no sense. The words mean what they seem to mean, but they are not, as Hoops thinks, savagely ironical.

49. Wrenn, ed., *"Beowulf" with the Finnesburg Fragment,* 209.

50. The nonspecific meaning of *druncen* without prefix may be implied by the existence of a number of derivatives which specifically denote "intoxicated": *fordrenct, fordruncen, ofdruncen, oferdrenced, oferdruncen, windruncen.*

51. The same implication may be present in 1467 ("wine druncen"), since the epithet "eafoþes cræftig" in the preceding line would seem to suggest that Unferth's flaw is that he lacks valor despite his having the physical strength necessary for brave deeds, not simply that he is a toper.

52. I quote Klaeber's text, as modified by Mary P. Richards, "A Reexamination of *Beowulf,* ll. 3180–82," *ELN* 10 (1973), 163–67.

53. E.g. in ll. 1480–81, 2529–33.

54. I am in agreement with Richards that the epithets in 3181–82a would have been perceived as Christian attributes, but I see the Christian senses coexisting with pagan ones, in the manner suggested throughout these

lectures. Cf. Bruce Mitchell, "Linguistic Facts and the Interpretation of Old English Poetry," *Anglo-Saxon England* 4 (1975), 28.

55. Stanley, "Hæthenra Hyht in *Beowulf,*" 147–50, discusses *lofgeornost* with insight and accuracy. Cf. Whitelock, *The Beginnings of English Society,* 27.

56. For my rendering of *wundor,* see Stanley, "Hæthenra Hyht," 138.

INDEX